RELATIONSHIPS

RELATIONSHIPS

Edited by Bob Williams
Photography by Jessica Crespo

SHOWTIME BOOKS
STATEN ISLAND, NEW YORK

Published by Showtime Books
140 Sheldon Avenue, Staten Island, N.Y. 10312
bwshowtime@aol.com

www.showtimepublications.com

First Printing — November 2017

Cover photo by https://pixabay.com/de/users/TeroVesalainen-809550/ [CC0], via Wikimedia Commons

ISBN 978-0-9911860-3-7

Photography by Jessica Crespo
Book design, cover and interior layout
by Kitty Werner, RSBPress

Text set in Minion Pro and Century Gothic

To

Dovid

Contents

Foreword

Was there ever a moment in your life when you suddenly realized you had become successful?

In my business and entertainment careers here on Staten Island, I've always thought that if people were money, I'd be a billionaire! Why? Because when I meet someone I immediately have networking and relationship building in mind. I have personally networked for the past five decades. That's a half century! Fifty years! And from the beginning I understood one very important business idiom: networking and relationships inevitably lead to business success. Simple as that!

You see, I realized early on that if I hoped to be successful in business, my potential customers would need to know who I am, where I am, and how they could reach me. We call this branding.

Make no mistake. Branding doesn't occur overnight. It's a lengthy process that takes a lot of time, money, integrity and quality behavior.

The 13 contributors to this book — a baker's dozen plus one, so to speak — are successful Staten Island business persons. As such, they certainly understand the importance of networking and relationships. And in the following pages they share their valuable thoughts, insights and business strategies.

I hope you enjoy their contributions!

Al Lambert
November, 2017

Here's to the crazy ones. The misfits. The rebels. The troublemakers. The round pegs in the square holes. The ones who see things differently. They're not fond of rules. And they have no respect for the status quo. You can quote them, disagree with them, glorify or vilify them.
About the only thing you can't do is ignore them. Because they change things. They push the human race forward. And while some may see them as the crazy ones, we see genius. Because the people who are crazy enough to think they can change the world, are the ones who do.

— *Steve Jobs*

Sonia Golden
Golden Key Interiors

Building Relationships

By definition, networking is the exchange of information or services among individuals, groups or institutions — specifically, the cultivation of productive *relationships* for employment or business. How do networking and relationship building relate to one another? I believe that effective networking is all about building trusted relationships. Successful business people know that networking and relationship marketing are more about nurturing or farming than they are about hunting. It is about building connections with other professionals who are here to stay. If you are collecting names or business cards, chances are your networking strategy needs an overhaul. Following are some strategies for concentrating on quality rather than quantity, which ultimately is how you will land that new client. In this deeply networked world it's important to pay attention to how we connect and manage our networks. Here, then, are suggestions for building more genuine relationships through networking:

First. Be a good gatekeeper. Whether it's via Linked-In or Facebook, do not accept a connection request from anyone to whom you are not personally connected. Yes, if there are only two of 10 people doing certain work, and you are one of them, then accept the connection. That's the exception to the rule. Otherwise, you really need to know who someone is before you accept the invitation. Connections to people we know tend to keep the relationships real. If you do meet someone with great expertise in your area, by all means keep the connection active and reciprocal.

Second. How many email newsletters do you normally receive? What percent of the total do you actually read? Understand that email newsletters aren't about connecting. They are about advertising. Next time you receive an email newsletter about a new report, a piece of research, a tool or an event, try this technique: ask yourself, who would find it valuable? Then forward the email to that person or persons. These forwards will inevitably result in some conversation. They will help people remember who you are, and they communicate to contacts that you are thinking about them.

Third. Have some sharable ideas. Try this. Think of three interesting ideas. Now keep these three ideas in your mind. Current events and popular topics work well. You see, these ideas will act as a springboard when you meet someone for the first time. You can open up a dialogue, which is an important first step in beginning a relationship.

Networking and relationship marketing are fairly new concepts. From the mid-1980s to the 90s, systems and structures began to emerge that shifted a lot of business owners from the single minded focus of direct selling to a broader scope, which included networking and relationship marketing. There are a few different ways to network. Some entrepreneurs do best by joining online groups that specialize in a sole product. Others join lists of people in different categories. These lists also provide ratings for the potential client. Face to face networking is yet another method. Each system works. What works best for your business or profession is a matter of experimenting with all three. For me, face to face networking is the most successful method. I'm an interior decorator, and many people initially have certain fears when it comes to interior decorators. They might feel that we are expensive, or that we will take over the project and not allow enough input from them. By seeing me on a one-on-one basis, or in a group, it helps people to be more comfortable with me. They find out that I am fair and that I always look out for the interests of my clients. When you are thinking of building a network, ask yourself a question: why would people want to network with me? Networking isn't just about what you are going to get, it is also about what you are going to give to others. Take a good hard look at what you can offer as an effective networker. Are you willing you consistently spend time and energy building and nurturing your professional network? Networking is a powerful marketing tool when it is a win-win for everyone. As with any element of profitable marketing, you must have a realistic understanding of how networking fits into your overall business building plan. What is your networking objective? How will you measure networking success?

Don't go to networking functions as a wandering generality. Know what you want to accomplish, why you want to accomplish it and how you are going to accomplish it. In other words, what is your networking goal? Networking is for the long haul. You will grow your business and develop relationships based on trust and respect. Some relationships develop quickly. Others take much longer. So the business building goal should be the solid relationships that result.

Relationship marketing involves building deep networks with other people strongly rooted in a connection that is developed over time. Relationships don't just spring up full grown. They must be nurtured. They grow, fed by mutual trust and shared benefits. They develop with three facets: visibility, credibility and value. Every relationship is different depending on the individuals involved and how they relate to each other over time. It starts out slowly, each individual discovering what the other has to offer. With time, commitment and familiarity, relationships mature and trust develops. This kind of relationship is mutually rewarding and self-perpetuating. Years ago, when I was looking to join a networking group, I first visited many groups. I noticed the members' tone and attitude and whether or not they supported each other. Was the leadership competent? Ask yourself what your goals are in participating in a networking meeting so that you will pick a group that will help you get what you are looking for. Some groups are based on learning, making contacts, and/or volunteering, rather than on strictly making business connections.

When a new person joins my business networking group, Business Guild II of the Staten Island Chamber of Commerce, he or she communicates with the others and starts to establish links with other members. The more contact you have with the group individually and as a whole, the greater your visibility. The more you are seen and heard, the more other members accept you as someone to whom they can or should refer business. With time, they begin to give you business referrals. If expectations are fulfilled and they are satisfied with the way their referral was handled, credibility develops. Credibility grows with interaction with the group and as others accept that you are good at what you do. There are other opportunities that arise from networking, such as joint ventures, partnerships and speaking and writing opportunities. Being visible is a big benefit of networking. Another benefit is increased confidence. Regular networking encourages you to talk to people. As a business owner, your business growth is dependent on how well you represent yourself. Being able to talk in front of people is an extremely important asset.

As time goes by, members consider the value of their membership in the group. Is this a group that helps you grow as a business person? Information is exchanged at every meeting. Each person brings something different to the table. Sometimes it is a discussion of new rules affecting business in general, or a new way of handling an issue, or an always valued client referral. It does not take the same amount of time for each person to develop and get the most out of their attendance. People first need to get to know you, then get to like you, and finally get to trust you. A successful member knows that it is important to have a mindset that allows you to give as much in time and effort as you expect in return. The business building goal is not in collecting business cards but in the solid relationships that result. There are social activities as well where members meet less formally and develop stronger relationships. Many friendships form as a result of networking as we are all like minded business owners who want to grow our businesses. We meet regularly — and, hopefully, trust develops, so naturally over time strong friendships tend to form.

I have been an interior decorator for more than 30 years. As a new decorator, I needed to meet as many people as possible and let them know what I do and how I work. The quickest way to build a strong business is to find people who know a lot of other people, and then show them what you do. These people are called centers of influence. They are people who know and trust you and would recommend you because they know you are good at what you do. As I was developing my craft and learning more about design, color and space, I was also developing centers of influence. There are many people who are friends, former or ongoing clients, business associates, and complimentary businesses that have been referring me for many years. The reverse is also true. You need to become a powerful resource for others. When you are known as a strong resource, people turn to you for suggestions, ideas and names of other people so that you stay visible to them. When I first joined the Chamber of Commerce I attended many mixers. One day, in a Staten Island diner, I joined a few people who were starting a networking group

Sonia Golden, known by all as Sonny, has been an interior decorator for more than 30 years. She volunteers in her community as president of her temple sisterhood. Sonny says she loves to travel, see a good play, learn history and talk politics. An ongoing pleasure, she says, is socializing and cooking for family and friends. sonnygolden@msn.com that allowed only one of each kind of business to join. That developed into Business Guild I. I stayed with that group for years until a family member developed some health problems and needed my help. When that resolved, I looked again for a new networking group. I went to quite a few meetings with different organizations, and finally I found a home in Business Guild II. The people were friendly and open. In short, I felt I was able to relate to them. The local business guilds have become so popular that now three of them exist. As I said, I belong to Business Guild 2. I like the people in the group, and I trust and refer people to them.

I also conduct workshops at different venues, informing participants of the current decorating trends and colors. It is important for me to be viewed as an expert in my field so that people turn to me for advice. For example, when LED lighting was being developed, and was still fairly new, I conducted seminars on how a homeowner could choose the right LED lights. I try to show people how to create their own unique style. I've conducted seminars on different topics: for example, color and how it affects you; how to begin decorating a home or office; buying art and where to hang art; how to decorate for the holidays; developing a personal style; current decorating trends; how to choose colors for your own space, and more. Local home shows are other ways to meet new people and eventually to make more centers of influence. I've given lectures at various well-attended home shows. My photograph even appeared in the newspaper for these, usually with an accompanying story. Charitable organizations are always looking for speakers, and I am usually most willing to help. I enjoy meeting new people and I believe they enjoy meeting me. In any service business, visibility is important. The more people know about me and what I do, the more possibilities I have to get new clients, and centers of influence are out there for me and in turn new relationships.

As Aristotle said, "Say nothing. Do nothing. Be nothing."

Simply, you must take action if you hope to be noticed.

Joe Sollitto
AAMCO Transmissions

Cultivating Relationships

Networking has helped my career and my business in many different ways.

According to the Merriman-Webster Dictionary, networking is "the exchange of information or services among individuals, groups or institutions; *specifically*: the cultivation of productive *relationships* for employment or business." While individuals seek to build relationships for a personal gain, everyone involved in networking will mutually benefit from working together. Networking is the most valuable skill a person in the business world can possess.

I am by nature a shy and quiet person and admittedly not comfortable socializing in large groups. But I understand that to have the success I want, I need to continuously focus on cultivating relationships — even if I am not comfortable doing so. I appreciate the value of networking, and I understand that networking is a function of one's effort. The more a person puts into networking, the more that person will get out of it.

The importance of building relationships was evident to me early on in my professional career. My first job after graduating college was in the emerging markets operations department of J.P. Morgan. It was an area of which I had little knowledge, so I needed to quickly educate myself. I read books. More importantly, though, I took every opportunity to meet and speak with colleagues. Through my conversations, I not only learned a lot about the financial products with which I was working, but I developed several strong relationships. Eventually, after almost two years of working in that entry position, I started to look for another job within the firm. I reached out to several people in other groups with whom I was indirectly working, and I expressed my interest in joining them. A few different opportunities were available; but I decided to pursue a different route.

Linda, one of my co-workers with whom I had worked closely, had left our team for another department within the company several months before my search. She had transferred to the risk management department, which was an area I had more interest in than my current department. So I contacted her and asked if there were any positions available in her new group. Linda said she wasn't sure, but she recommended I meet with her group's team leader, a vice president, also named Joe, from Staten Island. I scheduled a meeting with Joe to discuss my background and any potential opportunities within his group. We had an excellent conversation and Joe said that although there was not an opening within the group, he would keep me in mind when one did occur.

That opportunity came much faster than I had expected. I received a call the following week from Joe asking me to come in for a formal interview and meet other members of the team. There were some structural changes occurring in the group that Joe said he couldn't mention at the time, but he said he wanted me to join his team. He said that Linda had spoken very well about me and he trusted her opinion since he was impressed with her work. About a month later I started in the risk management group where I worked for two years. Eventually I left the firm to return to college full time to pursue a Master's in Business Administration.

Interestingly, throughout my two-year stay in business school, the emphasis was on the importance of networking. The school often put its students in situations conducive to networking and interaction. Many events were dedicated specifically to networking among fellow students, faculty and special invited guests. During my time at business school I developed strong relationships with many classmates I could call upon for professional help. However, the school's emphasis on networking did not end at graduation. Frequent alumni functions, such as networking cocktail parties and presentations, continue to this day to bring together graduates and foster the relationship-building atmosphere.

Here's another example. At one point in my life I was between jobs and I was searching for a new opportunity in finance. I was only two years out of business school, so I contacted other alumni for help in my job search. By the way, an alumni network is an excellent resource and basis for networking. The common bond inherent in attending the same school is valuable. This relationship makes initial contact easy, and it certainly opens doors. This is especially true in the job search where having a contact to help you get your foot in the door is an enormous advantage over the competition. Through my contacts, I had earned several interviews — but I did not receive an offer that excited me. So I continued to reach out to alumni and other contacts. Lo and behold, it was an unexpected person that helped me into the next stage of my career.

It is often said "it's not what you know but who you know." A better adage is "it's not what you know but who you know and *who they know*." Listen to this. One day I met an old friend and one of his friends, John, whom I knew casually. The three of us spent the afternoon hanging out. During our conversation I had mentioned that I was looking for another job. It was just casual banter on a spring Saturday. John suggested that I send him my resume so he could share it with a friend who was "doing well with some accounting firm in the city." John was living in Las Vegas at the time. I really didn't think he could help me, but I sent him my resume anyway.

A few weeks later, bingo! I received a phone call from Deloitte & Touche, one of the country's Big 4 accounting firms. Its financial valuation services group had received my resume and invited me in for an interview. I thought that maybe an employment agency had sent my resume to them, but I soon realized that it was actually John's friend who received my resume and helped get me the interview. The result: I received a job offer! I discovered that John's friend was a senior manager in the firm and was one of John's close friends from high school. From that moment, I learned never to underestimate anyone or the power of their network.

I stayed with Deloitte five years. Then I began working full time with my family in our auto repair business. One of my priorities there was to grow sales through community networking. I researched options and I decided to join Business Guild 2 of the Staten Island Chamber of Commerce. The guild is a networking group that meets weekly. We discuss ideas, exchange business tips and referrals, and promote each other's business. In Staten Island, where our business is located, relationships — that is, who you know — are important. And they carry a lot of weight. Despite a population of nearly a half-million, Staten

Island remains a close knit community with few degrees of separation. Cultivating and maintaining strong relationships are critical for business success in Staten Island, and my business guild has been a vital ingredient in our efforts to grow our network and sales there. From the time I joined the guild, we have seen a steady increase in revenue and in our customer base. We have become a trusted source of auto repair within my networking group and we have gained several guild members as loyal customers.

While increased revenue is often thought to be the primary goal of business networking, a second important goal is to gain information and eventually to learn. My brother Anthony is my business partner, and we both acknowledge that there are many smart people in the industry — people much smarter than we are. Anthony is constantly brainstorming new marketing ideas. His favorite source of ideas is fellow repair shop owners. Anthony is more outgoing than I am. So he has no problem telephoning a fellow shop owner he might have read about in a trade magazine to discuss industry issues — and thereby educate ourselves. We are members of several industry groups, and we frequently attend meetings to speak with other industry professionals. We have developed excellent contacts in the industry and have learned and implemented many innovative tools to grow our business. Some of our marketing techniques for acquiring and retaining customers have been adopted by other AAMCO shops in the chain. It is often said that knowledge is power. For us, networking to gain information is as important as networking to gain direct sales.

Much of my professional and personal success can be attributed to the relationships I cultivated over the years. Whether it has been to learn or to earn, networking and developing relationships have been — and will continue to be — important parts of my life.

Joe Sollitto is a native Staten Islander who lives in Brooklyn with his wife, Rebekah, daughter, Rosalie, and son Charles. He enjoys cooking, reading, walking around New York and spending time with his family. Joe is a passionate Mets, Jets and Knicks fan awaiting patiently for a championship.   statenislandaamco@gmail.com

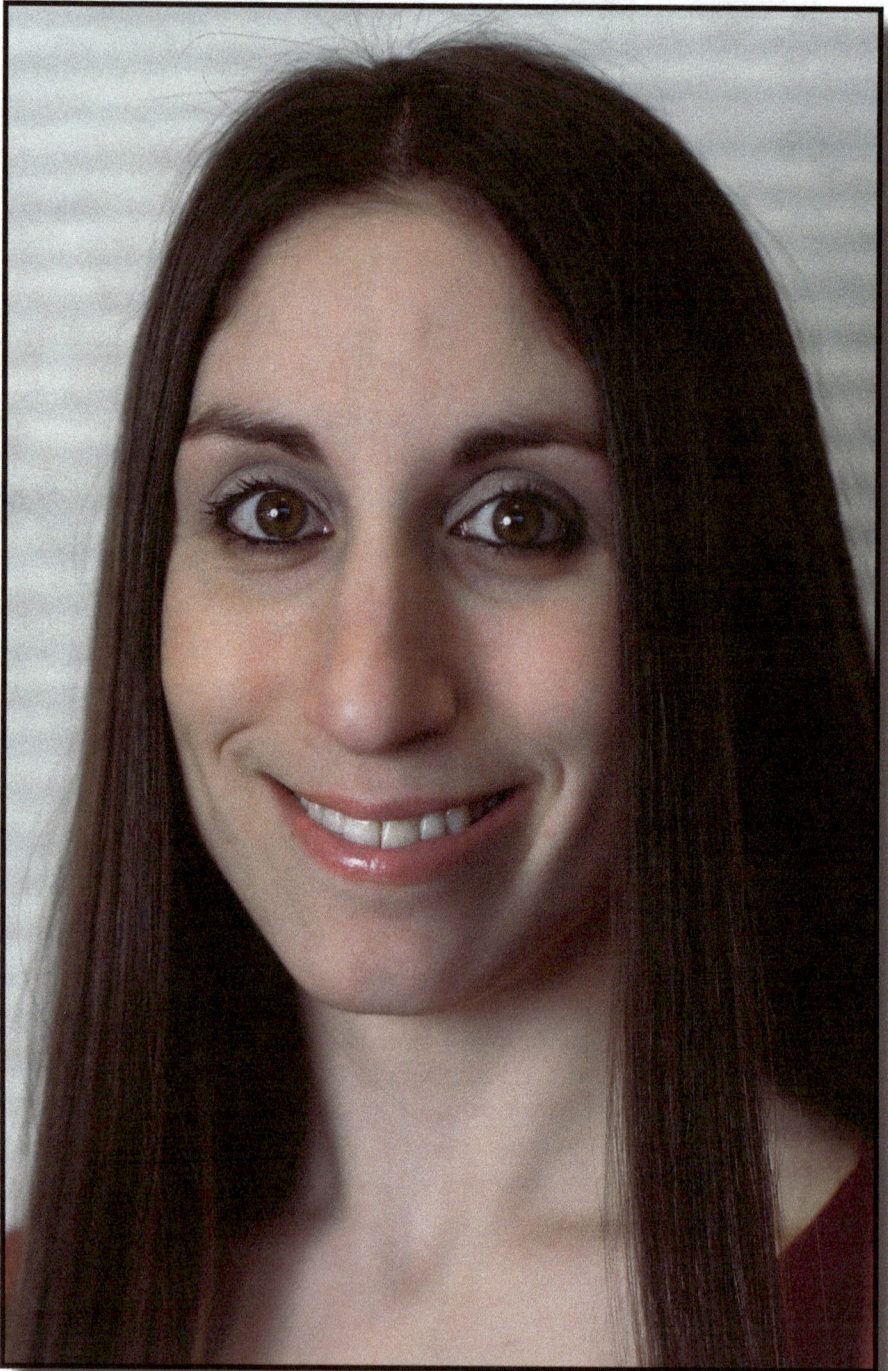

Cristina Occhipinti
Certified Public Accountant

The Strength of Relationships

I was born in 1984, so I possess some common characteristics of the millennial generation. Characteristics such as moving at a rapid pace ... expectations of immediate responses ... being technologically savvy ... constant involvement with social media ... wanting more work-life balance ... and minimal face-to-face interaction. Even though I share most of these traits, qualities outside this demographic have led my past relationships to develop into successful new business opportunities. Four of these best practices that I would like to share are: a) connecting with people, b) never burning bridges, c) the power of listening and providing exceptional communication to clients, and d) the strength of networking and *relationships.*

Let's talk about connecting with people.

During my junior year at Wagner College I earned a summer internship at PricewaterhouseCoopers, LLP ("PwC") in Florham Park, N.J. Just before the internship program began, PwC hosted a "welcome interns" social event. Attendees included new interns, such as myself, and the partners and staff from PwC's Florham Park office. I remember when I walked into the room. There was an overwhelming sea of people who appeared to know one another. I knew no one. Wagner was a relatively small recruiting college for PwC, so I was the only Wagner intern at this event. Most of the other interns were from larger colleges. Many had met before. As I walked to a table, the first person to greet me was Stephen Murphy, a PwC partner in the tax department. He was from the same team I would be working with as an intern. So, naturally, we began talking, and I quickly learned that he was originally from Staten Island. Like myself, he remained on Staten Island for college. Thus, we had made a strong initial connection because of the Staten Island history, roots and background that we had in common. I was relieved at how comfortable he made me feel because of our common ground -- especially since I didn't really know anyone there. Although I only had limited interactions with Mr. Murphy during my summer internship, I knew I'd be connecting with him in the future because I had been given a full-time PwC position. A few years after I began working full-time at PwC, he and I did, in fact, meet again. We worked together on the same project, so I was able to showcase my accounting and tax knowledge. At the same time, I advanced our relationship. Just recently, he called me and presented me with a business opportunity. He asked if I would help a colleague with the tax and accounting responsibilities necessary to start a new company. This was more than 10 years from the time we first met, and after I had already left PwC. I was thrilled that my relationship with him led him to recommend my accounting services to his contacts. Although this new business opportunity didn't materialize right away, I was able to gain a new client. That's a client I still work with today. This new relationship is now yet another connection that can lead to more business.

Now we arrive at bridges. A lesson that my mother always preached was to never burn bridges. While this is a cliché, it is indeed an important and significant cliché. I'm a Certified Public Accountant, so I can acquire new clients from anywhere. I realize, however, that it is often a connection to my past that leads a client to me. Today, with social media platforms easily available, it's much easier to communicate with contacts from your past. So my mother was correct when she insisted I never burn bridges with the people I meet. Today, I have two clients, both of whom I met years ago when playing soccer. At that time, I would have never imagined that today, nearly 20 years later, I would be helping them with tax preparation.

I'd like to tell you why I believe listening is so powerful in business.

I received an email one day from Nicholas F. Bellizzi of Canine Fence of Central New Jersey. "Your professionalism and good communication were paramount to you earning my business," he wrote me. He went on to say that's why he chose me to be his new accountant. Although Nick Bellizzi was not someone directly connected to my past, I did, indeed, learn important lessons from people in my past. The result: I was able to earn new business for myself. The two key lessons I learned, and I pass on to you, are the power of listening, and of providing exceptional communication to customers. Before first meeting with a potential client, it's important that you research the business and industry to learn all necessary and relevant information. While research certainly is important, building a solid relationship with the client is important, too. Although relationship building isn't something for which you can prepare, the actions you take during an initial meeting can affect the outcome. I listen carefully to a potential client's needs for my services. And I listen carefully to how they describe their business. This careful listening — instead of doing all the talking — helps me meet a potential client's expectations. While at your client's office, observing the surroundings will also help form a solid foundation in your relationship. Once a meeting is over, it is imperative to have follow up communication. A follow up email or telephone call allows you to thank them for their time, and to recap the meeting. At most of my initial client meetings I'll request certain information that will help me better assess their tax situations. I always include the specific items I request in this follow up to ensure we are in agreement. Good business practices for exceptional communication include answering in a timely manner (even if it is just to acknowledge you've received their message); relaying information and updates that may impact their business; and proactively checking in to see if my assistance is needed. When these two lessons are woven into daily practice, it is easy to build relationships and foundations that allow your business to grow and thrive.

Finally, building a relationship is everything.

After my son was born I decided to work closer to home so I could spend more time with him. This choice not only gave me the work life balance I was seeking but also the freedom to be able to generate my own business. During this time, a good friend of mine told me of an opening for a CPA in a business networking group. Joining Business Guild 2 of the Staten Island Chamber of Commerce gave me the opportunity to grow my business and develop lasting friendships — and business relationships. From these relationships, I have increased my own clientele, and have helped others do the same. So, you see, membership in a networking group is most important, too.

I'm sure I have many years ahead of me in business. I'm confident that if I continue to develop business fundamentals — especially relationships — I'll be a successful Certified Public Accountant.

When not involved with ledger sheets and trial balances, **Cristina Occhipinti** stays busy at home with her husband Jon, son Robbie, daughter Adriana and Cavalier King Charles Spaniel Peanut. She enjoys baking, coaching soccer and watching televised Yankee games. cocchipinti@gilicetocpa.com.

Relationships
Are
Connections

Chris Caggiano
Grand Oaks Funding, LLC

A Table, Tent and Giveaways

I watched the nervous flick of the pen as she scratched her name across the line. She looked up at her husband with a nervous smile. It was returned with a smile more of pride than of uneasy energy. Thus, with their signatures, another young couple became the newest members of a select fraternity: New York City homeowners. Buying a home was perhaps the most important purchase of their lives. And it's my profession and passion these days to help them along their journey.

Every day I do the work I love. I help people achieve their dream — the American Dream — of home ownership. Make no mistake. It has certainly been a long road to get here. And, over the years, *relationships* have had a lot to do with my success.

Let's begin at the beginning. I'm a Brooklyn native and the son of an entrepreneur. I knew at an early age that I wanted to own my own business, because I watched my father, who owned and operated Amoco gas stations in Brooklyn and Staten Island. Growing up, I spent a lot of time learning about business while working under my father's watchful eye.

I graduated McKee Vocational and Technical High School in 1981 with a major in electrical studies, and I went to work right away for an electrical contractor. Before long, I landed my first real job outside the family business working for Local 3 of the International Brotherhood of Electrical Workers. I advanced to a journeyman electrician. And I became shop steward. I enjoyed handling employee issues that were related to labor agreement violations. As shop steward I became the eyes and ears of the union, and I was passionate about helping others. I spent many productive years in the electrical industry.

Eventually, though, I longed for another challenge. I wanted to remain a people person, so I thought I'd pursue a sales career. A close friend of mine, James Haskell, owned Bell Mitsubishi in nearby Rahway, N.J.

So, through my friend James, I went to work as an automobile sales rep. James was a great mentor. My new career offered many opportunities: not just a Mitsubishi dealership, but also Saab, Audi, Subaru, Hyundai and used cars — all well known auto brands through which to test my sales skills. It was a great time in my life, and I really learned a lot about selling. The vehicles, however, were just a format for what was to lay ahead. I spent a lot of time each day on the phones staying busy because I brought with me to auto sales the same skill set I had developed under my father's tutelage. My father had taught me that customer satisfaction is the key to success. So, as customers came into the auto dealership, there I was to greet them in a warm and friendly manner. I soon developed a rapport with each customer. Many of those initial meetings led to sales. It's a tradition in the car business that, upon your first sale, your fellow sales reps literally cut your necktie in half. For me, this happened on my second day on the job. I had hit the ground running!

I began to outsell the other salesmen. I worked steadily to satisfy my customers. And I gained valuable sales and financing experience. One day my manager said to me that if I could sell 20 cars in a month, I would get a brand new car to drive. I sold 24 cars that month! The next month a dealer license plate and a new car of my choice was my incentive bonus. I knew then that I would never give up that perk! Selling cars for me became as second nature as breathing. I drove a different car every month for the next six years. These cars, by the way, are called demos. A demo is a new car that has never been registered; consequently it is eventually sold at a discount because it has mileage. Looking back, I can say that working in the auto industry gave me a sound foundation for dealing with people.

I believe successful salespeople give that extra effort that turns potential customers into customers. Salespeople who focus on details by doing whatever it takes to win over a prospective customer distinguish themselves from the many others who don't go to any extra effort. I also think that if you label success as an *attainable* goal, you will never consistently remain successful. That's right, *never*. Here's why. You can only succeed if you learn all there is to learn about your product, your competitors and your own personal selling. Since this learning process is continuous, it's an unattainable goal. With good reason, salespeople should not consider success an *attainable* ending point — but an objective that will always linger slightly beyond their reach. This is how first-time customers become lifelong clients.

I spent a decade in the auto business. Then, one day, my life changed when my friend, Marlene Kruger, introduced me to Nicholas Palumbo, a mortgage broker at a company called the Money Express. Marlene saw me as a success in the mortgage field. After a few meetings with Nicholas, I realized the mortgage business was for me. It could be a great fit, I thought. So I left the auto industry.

Through my work in auto sales I already had experience in analyzing credit reports and working with lenders to obtain auto finance for my clients. I had learned so much in the auto industry that I felt I had an edge in the housing industry. The only difference now was the collateral: I was dealing with a house instead of a car.

As a loan officer at the Money Express I helped people get financing for their real estate needs. Wow! And I thought putting people in a new car was satisfying! The first time I helped someone get into a new home, I knew I had found mine. I looked back and I realized that all the work I had done in my life had brought me to this point. From starting out working for my dad and learning the fundamentals of customer care, through my labor union experiences, and then as an auto dealer. All of it had prepared me for the field I was entering — the field of home mortgages.

Now, as a loan officer, I realized that I needed to get my name out there, as they say, to draw business. I began to spend a lot of time going to community events simply to get exposure. I became involved in events such as street fairs. And I even began to fine-tune my speaking skills. Meanwhile, I was still doing business with members of Local 3. I continued to speak at Local 3's meeting hall in Queens and at clubs and organizations in Brooklyn and Staten Island. I believed that by combining what I knew from past careers I would be able to again help the members of Local 3 and the affiliate clubs. Instead of helping solve problems in the electrical workplace, as a shop steward, I would now help them buy homes. To this day — and I've been out of the electrical industry for 13 years — through my past relationships I'm still the person they call when they need mortgage help.

Before long I realized that If I could get my loan message out while I was building my network, I'd be able to help even *more* people. So I kept looking for groups and organizations to which I could speak. The more I looked, the more potential customers I found. My speaking engagements grew from occasional presentations in small rooms to crowded auditoriums several times a month. My message was always simple. I spoke about the importance of credit and how to maintain it.

Here are some relationships that I made when I was a loan officer. I was the trusted advisor to many organizations, places where others could turn for sound advice. After years of building relationships I have developed a network of clients who reach out to me when they or their friends need mortgage help. An important part of my business has always been establishing long-term relationships. These relationships grew to such an extent, that I was not only their advisor, but also their friend. They referred their family, friends and coworkers.

One day years ago I received a telephone call from Patrick Lam, a real estate agent who worked for Douglas Elliman, the large real estate firm. He said he had heard that I was able to successfully help clients with complex loans. He said he was referred to me by an agent I had helped in the past. He then asked me if I could help his client get financing for a Manhattan condominium on East Broadway in Chinatown. He told me he was having a hard time obtaining financing for his clients. I asked for details about the project and said that I would call his client. Before long I was successful: I closed that deal. Many similar complicated financing projects followed in the same Chinatown condominium. The building quickly sold out. My friend Patrick thanked me, and he said he would refer me to other real estate brokers and agents who were having similar difficulties in obtaining financing for their clients. This eventually turned into a lot more transactions. I was now a trusted loan officer who was helping real estate brokers and their agents obtain financing for their clients. I also began speaking to real estate firms about the many different loan programs that were available. This helped me grow my referral network even more.

Through my relationship with Patrick Lam, I met Dick Liao, a commercial mortgage banker for more than 30 years. He asked if I would help refinance loans for his bank. The lender was under a time limit. They no longer wanted to lend on constructions projects. I worked diligently to obtain the financing for the construction loan in Lower Manhattan. The loan closed the lender received their funds back and all was well. I was able to secure financing from a credit union in Long Island. I was called many times for several large projects, which was a real game changer.

Over the years, in my quest to find potential customers, I went to many evening and weekend events. At one, a street fair, I arrived with my usual professional tools — a table, tent and giveaways. Soon, a woman stopped and said she was interested in buying a home. She asked me a few questions, and we exchanged contact information. A few days later I called her to tell her that before buying a home she should be qualified for a mortgage. I told her that after this qualification process was completed, she would know the exact value house she could buy. I also told her that she would not be able to make an offer on a home until she had been qualified. I asked her if she had a real estate agent, and she said she did. So I contacted the agent. Together we successfully closed the transaction. Soon, that real estate agent sent me clients. The agent and I worked together many years. Then one day the agent told me that her church had been trying to obtain financing to convert a Bayonne, N.J., warehouse to a house of worship. Her church needed a construction mortgage loan. So I scheduled a meeting with the pastor, Cesar Pasinio, from Day by Day Christian Ministries. Day by Day Christian Ministries, I learned, was renting in nearby Jersey City, and had been seeking financing for about four years. So I went to work on the project — and again I was successful! The construction mortgage loan closed, the warehouse conversion began and I eventually helped successfully complete the project.

Working for the Money Express I was fortunate to gain valuable exposure to and knowledge of the mortgage industry. I worked there for four years, from 2004 to 2008. Then I moved to another company, Fort Funding, where I was a loan officer for five years. Finally, in 2014, I established my own firm, Grand Oaks Funding, LLC.

Over the years many events led to my success. I always realized I wanted to build relationships that would last a lifetime. Before I opened my own company I forged many of those relationships. As a loan officer

I attended *every* loan closing — and this gave me the opportunity to meet all the parties involved, including the real estate agents. This was the beginning of establishing relationships and building my referral network.

Michael Jordan said it perfectly: Some people *want* it to happen. Some people *wish* it to happen. But there are those who *make* it happen!

If you ask me, relationships certainly help make it happen!

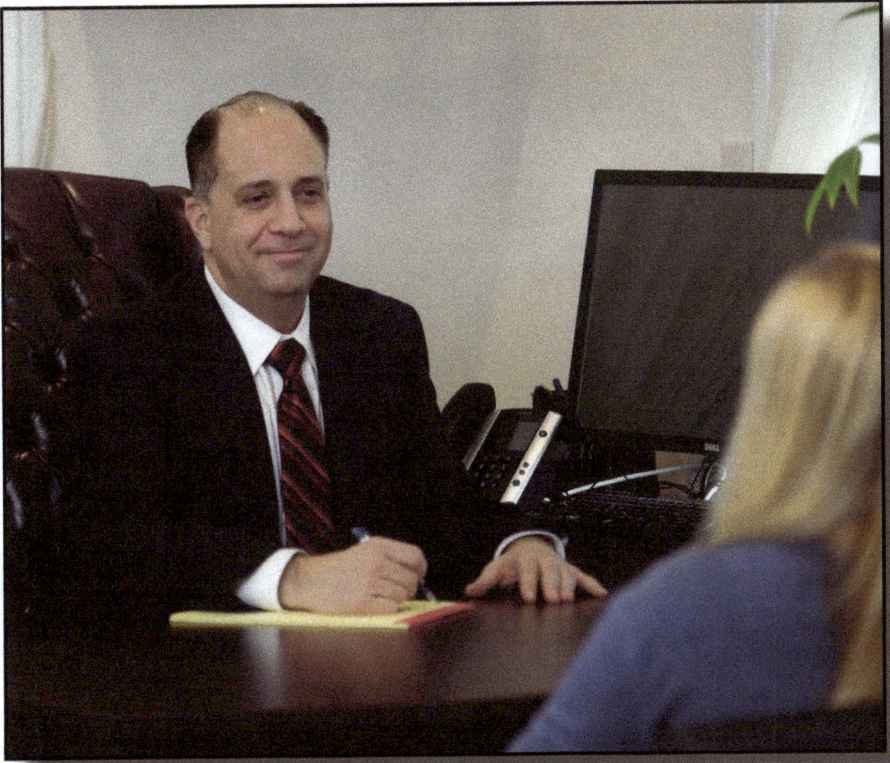

Chris Caggiano has been a licensed mortgage broker since 1997. chris@grandoaksfunding.com.

Chaka Blackman
Future Focus Consulting, LLC

The Right Connections

An African proverb comes to mind as I begin to write about how *relationships* lead to success. The proverb says: "If you want to go fast, go alone. If you want to go far, go with others."

I remember the first time I read this quote. I was preparing for a half marathon and was looking for inspirational material to guide my training. I knew that crossing the finish line after running 13.1 miles would require intense preparation and agility. Although long distance running is an individual endurance sport, I considered the physical and mental rigors associated with training for such a feat, and I decided to take a team approach. I turned to my husband and to my best friend for support.

My husband took on the role of coach and ran many of my early training miles with me. He also chose to enter a 5K race I had signed up for as part of my training plan in order to serve as my partner during the race. I can honestly say that he provided encouragement, feedback and positive reinforcement throughout my journey. Similarly, my best friend, who is an avid marathoner, ran my first half marathon with me. She helped me to persevere the last few miles when my body felt like giving up.

As I reflect on my journey, I realize how instrumental my husband and my best friend were in helping me to complete one of the most physically and mentally challenging experiences of my life. I am proud to say I completed my first half marathon in February, 2013. Indeed, it is high on my list of accomplishments. I even have the medal to prove it! As a matter of fact, I went on to run two more half marathons that same year.

I continued to reflect on the quote that was instrumental during my training. I now use it as a mantra that transcends most of my life domains. One of those domains is business. I have recognized that, in business, I can do well by myself, but I can accomplish the impossible with support and by making and maintaining great relationships.

My story is simple. I was born in Colon, Panama. Colon is rich in culture but significantly under-resourced when compared to the rest of the country. My mother decided to move to the United States in 1978; just she and I. I was a toddler at the time. We were able to move to the United States based on my aunt's status as an American citizen. In essence, my first major transition in life came about and was facilitated via a relationship. Had it not been for my aunt, my mother and I would not have been able to move to New York. The move meant a better life for both of us.

I lived in Brooklyn for more than 20 years, and I was able to stay focused on education based on my mother's influence and the influence of family, friends and teachers. I also developed my work ethic and was excited when I earned my working papers at the age of 15. Eager to help me obtain my first job, my mother picked up the phone and called my cousin, who was a manager at a fast food restaurant. He called me in for an interview the day after he spoke to my mother. On the day of the interview, I remember being nervous, since this was my first potential employment opportunity. We sat down in his office, and my cousin asked me about my approach to customer service, my time management and my ability to follow directions. At the end of the interview, he told me that I was hired. I was hired for my first job based on a relationship.

My mother always had a strong presence in my life when I was growing up and now as an adult. I think back to the many times she told me, "show me your friends, and I will tell you who you are." She was essentially telling me to be mindful of the relationships I chose as they would have an impact on my trajectory.

This summary of life experiences has helped me understand the importance of relationships and how important having the right connections are. I have countless examples of how relationships have shaped my life. My business is an extension of my life; therefore, I firmly believe that business affiliations and alliances have tremendous value. The right relationships do promote success!

I began my career as a high school teacher and then transitioned into the non-profit sector where I spent more than 15 years. Even though New York City boasts one of the nation's largest non-profit sectors, it remains a small environment where building bridges and maintaining relationships are both career imperatives. The sector is also known for having limited financial resources; therefore, the ability to network and build strong alliances is an asset. I have been blessed to have had great relationships with a variety of stakeholders including colleagues, school administrators, parents and students. There have been times I have had to call upon my relationships to expedite matters that could have slowed an important process. I have countless examples of times I was able to leverage relationships to bring quality services to children, young adults and families which include healthcare, educational enrichment, mentoring and recreational services.

One example of this: I have a former colleague who I have stayed in touch with over the years. He and I worked together as young teachers for the New York City Department of Education. We both moved on to other endeavors, but we have always stayed in touch. One day, we spoke about a new initiative I was planning to launch while at an organization for which I was working. I was a non-profit executive at the time. He mentioned that the New York City agency he was working for was researching new community-based organizations with which to partner. He said he thought it would be a good idea for him to add the organization's name to the list of potential service providers. Before I knew it, I received a call from his assistant commissioner. After a number of conversations, she decided that she was so impressed with the program model we were launching that she approved a pilot workshop at her facility. The pilot workshop meant that her young people could have access to our services. On the organizational side, it meant additional revenue and a new relationship. That relationship proved to be mutually beneficial during the initial pilot program and beyond. Had it not been for my former colleague, I would not have had a seat at the table with the assistant commissioner.

I have since left the non-profit sector and am now the founder of my own consulting firm. I help entrepreneurial dreamers start businesses, and I help start-ups build capacity through business and strategic planning. When I started my company, I knew I had access to the hundreds of personal and business relationships I had developed throughout my life and my career. As a part of my own business planning, I literally wrote down the names of everyone I thought could help me to propel my business forward. The list had hundreds of names on it. I also knew that my first client would come from a relationship. I began to reach out to everyone on that list to tell them about my new venture. I sent emails; I called people; I invited people out for coffee. After weeks of pitching, I secured my first non-profit client. I will never forget … that meeting took place at a local coffee shop a few blocks from my home in Staten Island. After outlining my business model and my value proposition, I landed my first client! My first client was the daughter of the Realtor who sold my husband and me our first home. Our Realtor knew how organized I was during the home buying process, so he decided to retain me to draft a business plan for his daughter's non-profit.

Since securing my first client, I have never looked back. I recognize that business is all about staying in touch with people and listening to what they want and need. I pride myself on maintaining long standing relationships with my clients, and I am always looking to build new relationships. Once again, to repeat that African proverb: "If you want to go fast, go alone. If you want to go far, go with others."

I want to go far!

Chaka Blackman founded Future Focus Consulting to ensure women and social entrepreneurs have access to the marketplace. She teaches graduate business courses at Southern New Hampshire University. cblackman@futurefocusnyc.com.

Jon Adamo
Phase One Construction

Question. Learn. Challenge.

As a child, I could never sit still nor, for that matter, pay attention. But these two character flaws apparently served me well throughout my life. I attended a strict Catholic grammar school run by nuns. That type of education made me develop a tough outer shell, to say the least. The nuns were not shy about instilling obedience in us daily, if you know what I mean. To receive this militaristic treatment at such a young age forced me to become regimented and stay alert. And you can bet I learned to pay close attention, too. This teaching style is banned today, but it did, in fact, serve a behavioral purpose in my day.

Because I was not able to sit still, I began to develop a curiosity about my surroundings and about the places to which I went. Sometimes this led me to new and different discoveries; other times it would simply get me into trouble. New discoveries were exciting and interesting; getting into trouble was not. However, when in trouble, one must defend oneself. By doing so, one hones his negotiating skills.

Once free of the primary school penitentiary, I moved on to St. Peter's Boys High School in New Brighton. St. Peter's was and still is an all-boys school run by the Christian Brothers. Not having girls in the school miraculously allowed me to actually pay attention for once in my young life. I joined both the cross-country and regular track teams, an experience that gave me an entirely new dimension of life. Luckily, I was used to running, so I had a pretty quick step. Remember, I had nuns in grammar school. I was Staten Island cross-country champion and was ranked a top runner in New York City and New York State. Our team was ranked nationally. I was captain in my junior and senior years. I have a collection of about 100 medals and trophies that I won in high school. I also won the prestigious Pepper Martin Running Scholarship Award, which paid my high school tuition. When I graduated I was offered running scholarships to a handful of local colleges. But after graduation I wanted to explore Europe educationally and culturally.

At 14, you see, I had visited relatives in France and the experience opened my eyes and mind to a new and undiscovered world. So, when I later graduated high school, I turned down the scholarships and instead packed my bags for what I thought would be a one-semester European educational and cultural extravaganza. I left the United States in the summer of 1988. My one-semester trip stretched into half my life!

I studied international relations at the American University of Paris, and I studied French at the Sorbonne. I had some of the best and most positive learning experiences of my life during the five years I spent in Paris. My university had 1,000 students from over 72 countries. Attending class was like being in an airport VIP lounge. I lived all over Paris, including on a friend's boat on the Seine—tied up directly in front of the Eiffel Tower; I lived across the street from the Louvre; and I lived on Avenue Grande Armee, with a window view of the Arc de Triomphe and Champs Elyesee. During those years I traveled extensively through Europe, visiting several countries more than once. I also took a six-month trip to explore cities and villages between Paris and Hong Kong, a journey that included travel on the Trans-Siberian Railroad. It was truly one of the most fascinating and culturally loaded journeys I had ever experienced!

During my last few months studying in Paris, a war in former Yugoslavia was just starting to kick off. I had been studying international relations, so I was keenly aware of the potential for an all out war. Unfortunately, this is exactly what happened a few months later. A school friend was putting together a logistical team for the European Community Humanitarian Office (ECHO) to travel to Yugoslavia to assess the on-ground humanitarian needs of refugees and displaced persons. We met, we spoke. I was in.

I packed quickly. Forty-eight hours later I arrived in a war zone. I spent several years during the war in Yugoslavia working for ECHO, ECTF (European Community Task Force) and UNHCR (United Nations High Commission for Refugees). I traveled widely in the country and spent several months in Sarajevo, Bosnia and Herzegovina. I also spent three years in Croatia where I served as Deputy Head of Mission for the Our Food Aid and Hygiene Project, which I helped develop and implement. We delivered more than 10,000 tons of food a month, and 750,000 hygiene packets to refugees, displaced persons and social cases in more than 700 refugee camps and centers. This first-hand experience of war, death and the humanitarian disaster it left in its wake has had a profound effect on my life, and it continues to have an effect to this day.

After the war, I needed some peace and quiet. So I decided to move to London to be closer to my son, Jack, who is British and who lived in the United Kingdom. I spent the next few years in Europe soul searching, traveling and visiting friends and family. I was lucky at the time to have invested all my wages in the stock market. That move now afforded me a comfortable stress-free lifestyle.

I became intrigued with wine during that period and decided I should learn everything there was learn about wine. So I studied wine academically, and spiritually, too! I nearly bought a vineyard in Croatia. It was in the town of Porec on the Istrian Peninsula overlooking the Adriatic Sea. But, as fate would have it, it was not my time. After a year of on-the-ground trips and bank and government negotiations, the deal fell through. Now, I was low on funds and I was back to square one.

In 2003, I decided to return to the United States to visit my family whom I had not seen in years. Once back in New York City, I thought I would reconnect with family and friends, and spend more time here in the United States. I had been overseas for nearly 15 years and had returned home to visit only four times. But I continued to jump back and forth to Europe; a few years ago I met Masha, the woman of my life who, as Mrs. Adamo, keeps me grounded and focused. This now allows me to nurture and grow my business.

It took time, but eventually I decided to pursue a career in the construction industry. Once I made that decision, however, I was thrown into the deep end, and I was forced to learn quickly. The only reason I believe I've had even a measure of success in this industry is because of my past life-experience educationally, professionally and personally. The construction business is more of a lifestyle. I sometimes work up to 16 hours a day, seven days a week. Customers call at all hours for advice, to review costs and contracts and even to change their minds about something upon which they had already agreed. Striking a balance between business and family life is, for me, the most important issue that I must master. Learning to say no to a customer or potential customer, or turning off the phone, is not easy—but sometimes it is necessary.

To be successful in the construction industry, a person needs good organizational skills, the ability to multitask and, certainly, a cool temperament. A person also needs unlimited patience, must be able to solve multiple issues, and must be honest, dedicated and humble.

If I had not been through so many challenging and difficult circumstances in my life that forced me to think outside the box, I doubt that I would have achieved the success I am blessed with today. I never stop learning or questioning what I am taught. I have a deep passion for education and I continue to challenge myself every day.

My business can be difficult at times, but I can't complain because it's what I do; I am proud and humbled at the same time. My advice to you: never stop questioning, never stop learning and never ever stop challenging yourself. You never know when you must dig deeply into your well of experience and knowledge. But when you do, make sure your well has not run dry!

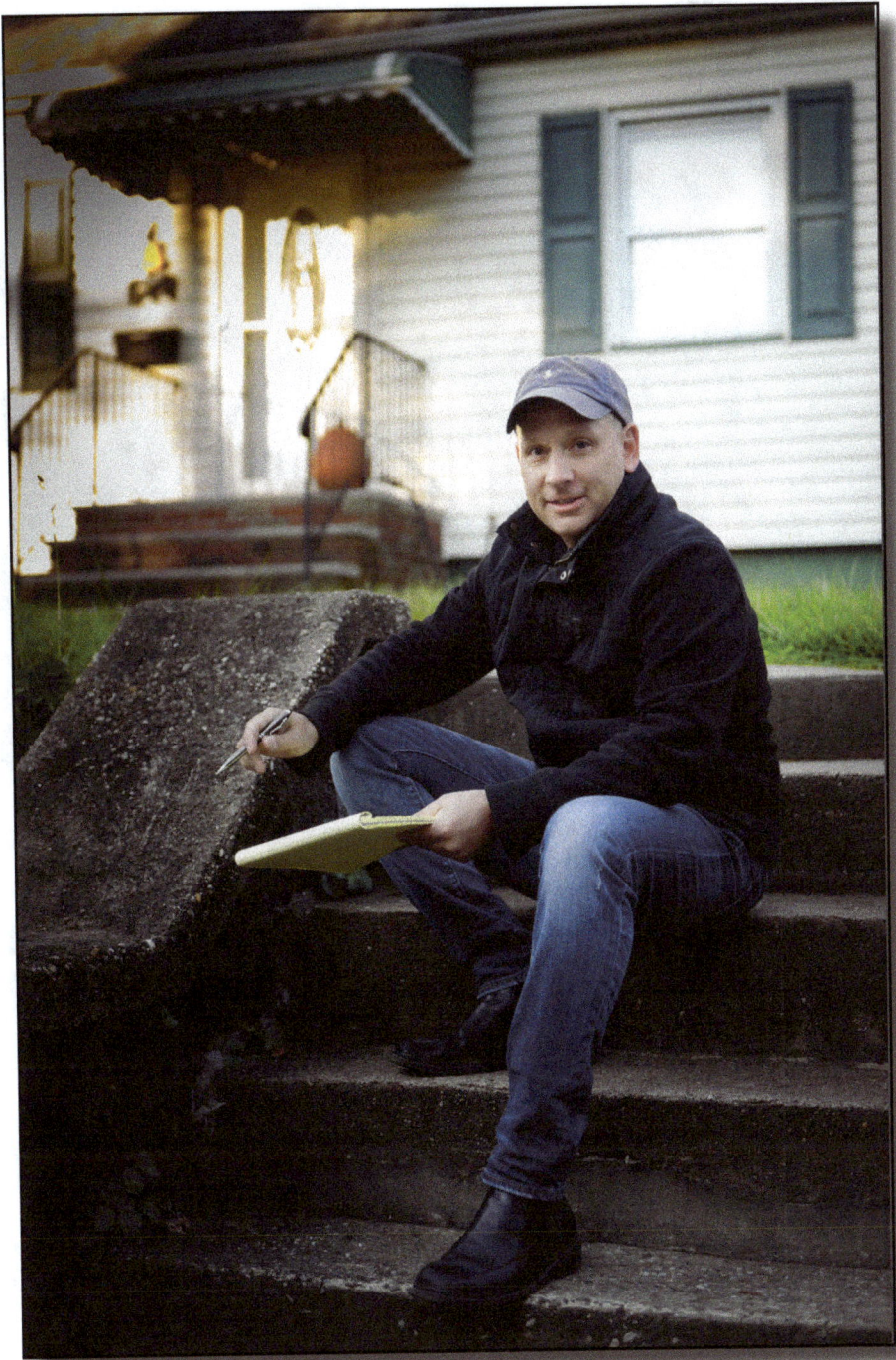

Jon Adamo grew up in Midland Beach. He says he's stunned to see the widespread destruction that Hurricane Sandy wrought to his childhood beachfront community. admin@phaseonenyc.com

Vik Cooper
Vik's Fine Jewelry

My Customer Comes First

When I came to the United States in 1989 as a young adult in my early twenties, I did not leave my home in Israel thinking that it would be the last time I would ever live there. I was not chasing the so-called American Dream. I came to this country, after serving four years in the Israeli military, simply for a vacation and to see what America had to offer, coast to coast. What I encountered instead was a life-changing experience, full of opportunities. While on my vacation here in America I decided to stay. Eventually I opened my own fine jewelry store, and have since only returned to Israel for visits.

When I first came to America, my plans were to travel from New York to Seattle, from Seattle to San Diego, and then back to New York by way of the southern states. I wanted to see as much of this country as possible in between. Once I arrived back in New York I realized that American culture was more like Israeli culture than I had expected, so I decided to extend my stay. Since I would be staying longer, it would be necessary to get a job to support myself. I found employment in the jewelry industry as a wholesaler.

After working as a jewelry wholesaler for several years, I realized that I wanted to lead a successful life here in America. The clear means to that end for me was to start my own business. So in 1990, at the age of 25, I did just that. I started with a small booth in the Jewelry Exchange in Caldor Plaza in Mariners Harbor. In time, I outgrew that small booth and moved on to a much larger space in the Coral Island Shopping Center in New Springville. I needed more exposure than I was getting in my small booth, and being in a shopping plaza at a busy intersection would give me a more prominent presence. Additionally, being in a larger space enabled me carry a larger selection of inventory and to serve my customers more comfortably. But after many successful years in the Coral Island Shopping Plaza, I felt it was again time expand my business. I relocated to my present location in the Heartland Village Shopping Plaza, my largest store yet, and could not be happier about it.

It was necessary for me to make these moves in order to provide my customers with the greatest selection of quality jewelry at the most comfortable and accessible locations possible. The fact that I have needed to move to a larger location twice in my career shows that my business not only sustains, it thrives. As I contemplate what it is about my business that has enabled me to grow rapidly, I can narrow it down to a handful of qualities: my experience in the Israeli military, my knowledge of the industry, my competitive pricing strategy and, most importantly, my dedication to customer service.

My experience in the military taught me discipline and dedication. These qualities were necessary in starting, sustaining and growing my business. Owning a business requires a routine full of dedication and discipline. It is necessary to work long hours, often six or seven days a week. Despite distractions, such as the desire to spend more time at with my wife and two children, the business requires sacrifice. While my military training taught me discipline and dedication, owning a business forced me to apply these characteristics to real life. The results certainly have led me to success.

Having a thorough knowledge of one's field of business is also extremely important. I spend a significant amount of time and effort keeping current with trends in my industry. I am always trying to keep my inventory unique, fresh and ahead of the curve. I make sure I know what brands my buyers are interested in and I make an effort to forecast what the next big trend will be. In order to do this, I attend various tradeshows each year, the biggest of which is in Las Vegas. At these shows, I meet with representatives from different brand-name jewelry manufacturers, and I am introduced to up and coming designers and artisans creating a more unique product.

For the past ten years my store has specialized in custom pieces. We design and manufacture custom jewelry for the client who knows exactly what she wants, or for the client who needs a bit of guidance to create a special one-of-a-kind piece. I myself do most of the design work. While we used to contract the manufacturing to outside specialists, we are now equipped to handle the manufacturing of these custom pieces on our premises. The ability to manufacture jewelry has given us a great advantage over our competitors, particularly when it comes to engagement rings. Manufacturing the jewelry on the premises not only enables us to create special pieces, but it enables us to keep our pricing competitive because we cut out the middleman.

Competitive pricing has enabled my business to grow, but this is mostly important because it serves to further my goal of providing the best customer service imaginable! The relationship I develop with my clients is extremely valuable. By providing my customers with the best price, I sell in higher quantity and I ensure that they will return to my store the next time they are looking for a piece of jewelry. I have customers who have been shopping in my store for 15 years. They sometimes stop in just to say hello. Because I know customers for so long, it makes them feel like family.

I treat my employees with the same familial attitude as well. My very first employee, Linda Metzger, still works with me. She left for a period of time to pursue work in another field, but knew she was always welcome to come back to my store. Sue Silverman, another employee, has worked with me for 12 years now. My customers know they can always walk into my store and see a friendly, familiar face.

This theory of treating our customers like family has made my store not just a place of business, but a comfortable, fun, enjoyable environment for me, my staff and my customers. There is no job too big or too small for us in the purchase or maintenance of jewelry. This is what keeps our customers happy and what keeps them coming back. We get to know them while they are browsing the showcases, waiting for a watch battery to be replaced, having a clasp fixed or having their jewelry cleaned.

When making a large jewelry purchase, such as an engagement ring or watch, or having repair, maintenance or cleaning performed on one's most valuable and prized possessions, it is necessary that the customer trusts the person with whom he or she is working. By forming these relationships with customers who come in for small jobs, we find they come back for large purchases as well. They then recommend us to their friends and family who are looking for a trustworthy jeweler. These friends and family will come in for small jobs and then, hopefully, for large transactions as well. The cycle continues — our client base grows.

The fact that my store has outgrown its location twice tells me that I am doing something right. While the dedication I learned in the military certainly helps oversee my daily operation, I attribute most of my success to my customers. I have worked very diligently to provide them with the best service possible and to provide them with the best selection, and this is what keeps them returning year after year. Certain aspects of my business may not transfer from one industry to another; but providing top-notch customer service is fully transferable to every industry. It is truly the key to my successful business.

Vik Cooper came to this country from Israel in 1989. He's been in the fine jewelry business ever since. Vik says he loves spending time with his immediate and extended families.

Relationships
Are
Affiliations

Bob Williams
Showtime Publications

Relationships = Success

Relationships. I learned early in my career that a *relationship* today could reap benefits tomorrow. Case in point: when David Rockefeller became Chase Manhattan Bank chairman. Right off the bat, Rockefeller scheduled a months-long tour of underdeveloped nations. Critics wondered why he was meeting and greeting leaders of obscure third world countries rather than concentrating on banking problems here at home. After all, they reasoned, no other major financial institution was eyeing poor nations. When he returned home, Rockefeller revealed his strategy. "No, these countries don't have the money for growth today," he explained. "But when they do grow and seek financing, we hope they'll turn to Chase." He was right. Over the years, country after country selected Chase for its financing. Leaders were unanimous in their reasoning: they had a friend at Chase Manhattan. David Rockefeller engineered a brilliant strategy. Certainly, it affected the bank's bottom line positively to the tune of millions of dollars. I always think about his strategy and try to emulate it when I can. Success, I learned, rarely comes quickly. Success, indeed, can result from a relationship.

Here's an example. Remember the 1970s film "Dog Day Afternoon," starring the actor Al Pacino? The plot was about two men who held up a bank and took the tellers hostage to get money for a sex change. In reality, the film was based on a true story: the armed robbery of a Chase Manhattan Bank branch in Brooklyn. I worked for Chase Manhattan at the time, and I was sent to the scene as the bank's press representative. Apparently, two men tried to hold up the bank, but somehow botched the job. Scared, they grabbed employees at gunpoint and were now trapped inside the bank. Police had the building surrounded. I found refuge in a small storefront beauty salon about four doors from the bank. The owner had allowed me to use her telephone (no cell phones back then), so I was able to keep in contact with my office. The beauty salon and its free telephone service drew a host of news reporters who realized they had immediate access to a bank spokesperson—me—and a phone line to their offices, to boot. They knew that official bank information about the holdup would come from me, so they stayed close. One reporter was Gerald F. Lieberman of *The New York Times*. Late in the day, about 5 p.m., he asked me if he could interview the bank manager when the hostage situation ended—assuming, of course, there would be no loss of life. He had a few hours, until 8:30 p.m., to make the *Times'* first edition for the next day. I agreed, and I told him to stay close by. So Gerry and I found a few comfortable chairs, loosened our ties and made ourselves at home in the tiny beauty salon—waiting for something to happen. Understand that the holdup began at about noon but didn't end until about 3:30 a.m. the following day—a space of about 15 hours.

To kill time, Gerry and I shot the breeze, talked about our jobs, our families, our schooling, our interests—anything and everything. Hours dragged on, but still nothing happened. Meanwhile, as we waited, the *Times* closed its first edition at 9 p.m., its second edition at 12 midnight and it's third and final edition at 2 a.m. There was even an extra postscript edition at 3 a.m. Gerry missed them all.

Then, at about 3:30 a.m. the two robbers walked out of the bank, released some tellers and forced remaining tellers at gunpoint into a stretch limo bound for La Guardia Airport. Police had promised that a private jet would fly them out of the country. As far as I was concerned, the hostage situation was over, so I drove home. Gerry, who had stayed with me through the night, never filed a story. He, too, headed home.

Hours later, at the airport, a police sharpshooter killed one of the robbers; the other man dropped his gun and surrendered. The bank tellers and their manager were unharmed.

Next morning Gerry Lieberman called me again with a request to interview the branch manager. I made a few telephone calls to pave the way, and Chase officials allowed the interview. His account of this bizarre bank holdup reached *Times* readers around the world. Gerry was happy to have finally written the story; I was happy to have helped him.

After that long night in Brooklyn, Gerry and I went our separate ways. But we remained friends. We had learned a lot about each other as we sat in that beauty salon waiting for a story to unfold. Indeed, we had developed a special relationship. Afterwards, Gerry often called me for help with a story he was writing. And every now and then I called Gerry with an idea I thought would be a great story for *The New York Times* readers. I remember the scenario: Gerry would listen to my pitch, then pause for a few seconds. "Sounds like a story, kid," he'd shoot back. "Let me check with my editor, then we'll have coffee and you can fill me in."

Over the years, as I became a successful public relations practitioner, I realized that my relationship with Gerry Lieberman probably had something to do with it.

Here's another story to illustrate relationships. I published a weekly newspaper in Long Island. As such, I handled advertising sales. A deli owned by an Indian man was located in my territory. The deli owner told me that his brother in Queens made advertising decisions. And, he added, the brothers were not interested in spending money to advertise. Nonetheless, I stopped in regularly for coffee and lunch and just to say hello. A few months passed and the owner and I began to chat. How's the weather? How about those Yankees! You know, the usual small talk. One day he tells me that his brother will finally advertise—but in the *Daily News!* This guy goes bananas with his brother. *"Daily News?* We cannot do that," he yells at his brother. "We know *Bob. Bob* is our friend. We must advertise with *Bob!"* Yep, I got the account. My newspaper carried his deli advertisement for years. The moral: a relationship = success.

Later, I sold advertising space for a newspaper group in the Bronx. That's right, the Bronx! One of my customers, a young man, advertised his business with me every week. He was happy because the ad helped him get business. One day I told him I was leaving the Bronx for a position in Staten Island. "No problem," he said. "Run my same ad in Staten Island." I replied, incredulously, "Joe, you don't understand. I'd love to carry your ad, but no one in Staten Island will travel all the way to the Bronx to buy your product." He looked at me, sadly. Apparently we had developed such a good friendship that he was ready to follow me to another location, completely out of his area. If you ask me, that's a relationship!

Finally, back to the Chase Manhattan Bank. Eventually, I left Chase for a greener pasture, but I remained friends with many co-workers, especially Fraser Seitel. Fraser and I had worked together in Chase's public relations department. He advanced to senior vice president in charge of just about everything. I became public relations and advertising director for the Boy Scouts of America, based here in New York. One day I was asked to put together a volunteer public relations committee. This committee would be comprised of top public relations, advertising and marketing people. They would give their time and talent to the Boy Scouts pro bono. Immediately, I thought of my old friend Fraser, the Chase Manhattan muckety-muck. Fraser agreed to serve on the committee. Then he went a step further: he offered to host our first committee meeting over lunch at Chase headquarters in Lower Manhattan. "We'll have it in David Rockefeller's private dining room," he added. Spectacular, I thought! I had by then recruited a dozen or so presidents and chairmen of top New York communications firms. Usually, few executives turn out for a routine committee luncheon. But let me tell you, this luncheon was different—with a capital D! Each and every committee member—and I'm talking big shots with shiny limos and uniformed drivers—made sure they attended that first luncheon meeting at Chase. Later, my superior wondered how I had pulled it off. I'm sure you know the answer. If you guessed that my longtime relationship with Frazier Seitel had something to do with it, you'd be absolutely correct!

My advice to you is simple: focus on relationships. For if you do, you stand to enjoy a most rewarding—and truly successful—personal and professional life.

Bob Williams first become interested in wordsmithing when he visited his father at work as a Linotype operator at the *New York Post*. Today, Bob has a passion for theatre, downhill skiing, public speaking and Harley Hogs. bwshowtime@aol.com

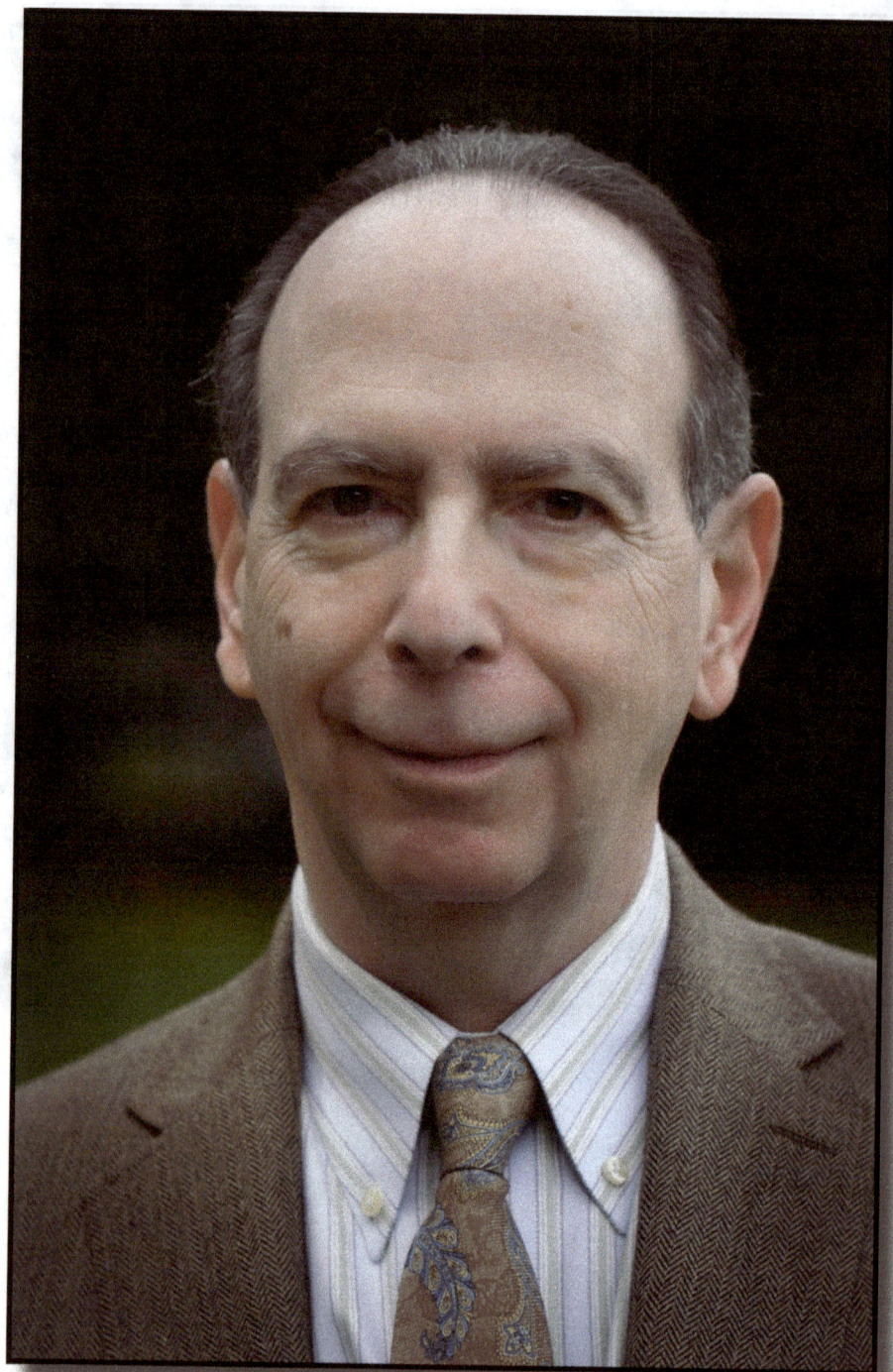

Norman N. Schwartz
Norman N. Schwartz Insurance Agency

Timing Is Everything

My first day as a Nationwide Insurance Agent was way back on November 22, 1992. My journey, as circuitous as it was, was definitely affected significantly by timing, and also by my desire to become a financial and emotional success. Looking back, I wonder how all the events connected to bring me to this point in my life.

I graduated Brooklyn College and headed for a career in teaching. My first assignment was as a fourth grade teacher. Later I moved onto teaching elementary physical education. It's here that I developed a gym leader program. I used 3rd, 4th and 5th grade "upper classmen" to help me instruct students in lower grades. Not only did the leaders love this opportunity, younger students enjoyed interaction with older students. It also gave the younger students something to strive for: to become a gym leader.

Each year the culmination of the gym leader program was our annual dance and gymnastic show. This presentation was an evening event where we showcased our accomplishments achieved throughout the year. The turnout was great and the leaders were rewarded for their hard work all year long. How proud I was!

But, as rewarding as my interactions and achievements were with the children, financially I always had to supplement my income with a second job. Here's where I had my first taste of the insurance business, among other occupations: real estate sales, Macy's sales, and car sales. Cars were always my first love, and I wound up at Safe Toyota on Coney Island Avenue in Brooklyn. I was teaching for 30 hours and selling Toyotas for 36 hours. Though I was doing well financially, I had no flexibility, and the long hours were taking their toll.

What I needed as a second job was something where I could supplement my income and also not be held to a fixed schedule. The insurance business seemed to be a perfect fit.

I enrolled in Baruch College's insurance brokerage program and then took the insurance broker's test. It was the hardest test I ever took. By some stroke of luck I passed. Thus began my first foray into the insurance business. Along with a partner, we began to sell all forms of insurance. We did have some financial success, but one thing about the insurance business is that you must be there for your policyholders. I was still teaching, and because I couldn't be there 100% for my policyholders we eventually sold our business. This experience was definitely worthwhile and it planted a life changing seed: I needed to concentrate on one career.

So, after 18 years I decided to leave teaching and focus my energies on one career where I hoped I'd be successful. Interestingly enough, I started out with my first love, automobiles.

I was able to find an opening at Bay Ridge Porsche, Audi and Volkswagen. It was a low key dealership with the main sale being Volkswagen. I spent a year there when a friend of mine called and said there was an opening in his dealership, Porsche-Audi Manhattan. He was the manager there and he told me this move would be a step up. It certainly was. The mainstay here was Audi—and a nice sprinkling of Porsches were in the mix, too. The bump in the road came when Audi started to fly through garages with unintended acceleration. Audi sales dropped. I saw the writing on the wall. It was time for me to move on. Fortunately, I found a position with David Michael Mercedes-Benz in Freehold, New Jersey.

Although these were positive experiences, the sales positions were totally commission-driven and owner-centered. As a sales person, I was at the mercy of management. Financially, I was doing well at Mercedes. But I was working a 52-hour week. One day our general manager told us during a meeting that he had good news for us. The good news was that we were going to a six-day work week! We'd have only one morning and one afternoon off. This wasn't for me. So I gave my notice.

Here's where insurance sales popped back into my life. While looking for a new job I came across a want ad for an associate agent for State Farm Insurance in Brooklyn. I interviewed for the position, got the job and spent two years there. Unfortunately, even though I was the production leader, a familiar problem popped up: it wasn't my own business. Again, time to move on.

Later, a fortuitous ad caught my attention as I was scouring *The New York Times* classified: Nationwide Insurance Agent wanted. Could this be the opportunity I was hoping for? I answered the ad and found out it was for an associate agent. Not what I was expecting, but something told me to go for it anyway.

The agency was located in Richmond Hill, Queens, and the agent was Tony Marino. I interviewed with Tony three times. Finally, after the third interview when I showed him my production he said, "Norman, I'm never going to make you happy." I then asked him how I could become a Nationwide agent with my own agency. To his credit, he then made a life altering suggestion. "Call my manager, Barry Hocheiser," he urged. Not only was the timing right, but I had the good fortune of meeting a great guy.

With Tony's blessing, I met Barry Hocheiser and was floored to learn there were no Nationwide agents in Staten Island. Which is why Nationwide was looking to put one here (timing?). I couldn't believe there wasn't an agent in Staten Island, but Barry explained there had been agents in Staten Island until the Verrazano-Narrows Bridge opened. With the influx of people relocating from Brooklyn, Nationwide couldn't raise its rates fast enough. So the firm pulled its agents off the Island. Nice going.

I met all the requirements except for one. In my eternal wisdom I had let my insurance broker's license lapse. Remember when I said earlier this was the hardest test I ever took? Guess what? I had to retake the test! I didn't have to take the courses again, but the test was mandatory and required for the job. Needless to say the pressure was on: pass the test or don't get the job. Well, I studied and studied and I can proudly say I passed the test for the second time. The job was mine.

Off I go to Nationwide Insurance School in Columbus, Ohio, on November 23, 1992. The only problem was that I had to fly there. I'm a fearful flyer. I took my meds and got there without incident. I had a good time at school, learned a lot and by the time school ended all my classmates knew of my fear of flying. That brings us to December 11, 1992, the day I was scheduled to fly back to New York. That morning, Frank Amos said to me, "Hey, Norm, you hear about that Nor'easter?" I told Frank in no uncertain terms to please be quiet. Well, not quite the words I used.

I got to the Columbus airport and, boy, was I in for a shock! Frank wasn't kidding. All flights to New York had been canceled due to one of the worst Nor'easters in our history. Well, the all clear was finally given that afternoon at 3. I was treated to one of the worst flights ever. Read turbulence. But, there was a rainbow at the end of the storm: I was now the owner of my own business. I was a full-fledged Nationwide agent!

In my absence, my manager, Barry, had set up my office, or should I say room. For that's what it was, a room on the second floor of Richmond Homes in Bulls Head. It more than served its purpose. Now all I had to do was grow my business. Prospecting for business is key to the insurance business. It wasn't one of my strengths, so I set out to get help. I put an ad in the *Staten Island Advance* for a telemarketer. To my surprise I was deluged with calls for the position. In January of 1993 I hired Grace Snyder for the position. She's been with me ever since. With Grace's help, now as office manager, we grew the business. Lesson learned: surround yourself with good people and don't be afraid to delegate.

As you're probably aware, all is not peaches and cream. Challenges are always thrown your way. You have to be ready to deal with those challenges and try to use them in some way to your advantage. There were times when Nationwide, for whatever reason, stopped writing a particular form of insurance, i.e. homeowners. It forced us to switch gears and cultivate new relationships with general agents to fill the homeowner void. These relationships are still in play. They came in handy again when Nationwide adopted a coastal strategy last year because of Hurricane Sandy.

Twenty-one years flies by quite fast. I measure my success only in terms of how I feel about my accomplishments. I set out to be my own boss and help people protect their possessions and family. Of this I'm certain: mission accomplished.

Thanks, timing!

When not insuring peoples' lives and possessions, as he has for the past two decades, **Norman Schwartz** enjoys tennis, dining out, going to movies and shows, and listening to Motown and doo wop music. Couch potato television watching is high on Norman's list, too. schwarn2@nationwide.com

Jessica Crespo
Jessica Crespo Photography

Be Yourself

For a few weeks, as I tried to sit down to write my chapter for this book, I found that my husband, my two little girls or some other matter that needed my immediate attention would constantly interrupt me. I love my life, the chaos, and being the one to, in a way, hold it all together. And even though it does get exhausting, I wouldn't change a thing. Before now, I spent my life searching for a place where I belonged. It wasn't until I became a wife, a mother, and a photographer that I realized everyone out there is pretty much looking for the same thing, and pretty much feeling the same way. All of a sudden I felt less alone, and I started allowing myself to feel at home in the here and now.

Maybe I should back up a bit and tell you a little about who I am and where I come from. My parents are from Ecuador and I was born up in Westchester. I was still a toddler when they decided to return to Ecuador in order to be close to family. Life as a child in Ecuador was fun. There was plenty of room to run around, plenty of cousins to play with, and not a care in the world. However, I don't think it was the same way for my parents. I was four years old when my little brother was born and eight years old when they decided to move us back to New York because of economic reasons.

Things were not easy once we returned to Westchester. My father was a mechanic and had to work two jobs, so we almost never saw him. He would leave every morning as we were waking up for school and come home when we were getting ready for bed. He even worked half days on Saturdays. My mother worked a full-time job as well, so her time was also limited. We lived in rentals, watching every penny and buying clothes at the local Salvation Army thrift store. At school, I felt insecure. I couldn't relate to my classmates who always seemed to have the latest and greatest. Unfortunately, my parents did not know how, nor did they have the time, to help us socialize with our peers outside of school, or even attend most school functions. My classmates would talk about their vacations to Disney every year like it was just around the corner. I admired how lucky they were, but felt inadequate because I could only dream of going someday. I not only dreamed of going to Disney, but I dreamed of going on any family vacation at all.

Three years later, my parents decided to move back to Ecuador after my grandfather passed away. Life in Ecuador seemed easier again from a kid's perspective. There were cousins to play with and classmates who admired the fact I came from the United States. It took some adjusting but I felt accepted and included—as if how I was perceived came from others and not from within.

The economy of Ecuador has always been unstable and my parents worried constantly about providing for us. We tried to make it work for five years, but in the end my parents decided to come back to New York. By then I was 16 and half way through high school, so saying goodbye to all my friends, family and the life I knew and loved was truly heart breaking. My parents returned to the life of working non-stop and I returned to feeling inadequate around my peers. I didn't understand why it was so difficult or why I felt so alone. Eventually, leaving for college seemed like it would be a relief, a new start, but as it turned out, it was just the beginning of more confusion and bad decisions on my part.

I started life at SUNY College of Geneseo in the fall of 1997, and even though I made a few friendships, I never felt like I belonged. During my first two years there I went from being an A student all my life to being a mediocre one. I decided to take a break and found an international volunteer program that would provide room and board. Thanks to my language skills, which at the time felt like the only thing I was consistently good at, I was assigned to Rome. I know, a dream come true! And yes, for a year, I had no worries and no pressures to fit in. I was away from a place where I had to force myself to belong and was instead able to just be who I was.

When I returned to the United States, I gave Geneseo one more try. I switched majors to politics from biology and, although that first semester showed some promise, my studies suffered again during the second semester. I felt like the biggest disappointment to my parents, who didn't know what to make of what I was going through. I started 2002 by withdrawing from Geneseo and going to work as an associate for an international moving company. I quickly learned, through real life experience, that I had little chance of being taken seriously without a college degree.

By the spring of 2003, I had had enough and was ready to start anew. This time I was determined to get my college degree as soon as possible. I began classes at Manhattan College. I took as many classes and internships as I could each semester, including summers. It worked. I made the Honors Enrichment Program and graduated Magna Cum Laude with a 3.8 GPA and double major in economics and global business studies. I finally began to feel proud of myself again and was finding courage from within to take on future obstacles. At this point, I had an idea that I would like to someday become an entrepreneur, but I was not yet clear on details.

After college, I spent about five years in the corporate world. At first, I took a job in Manhattan's financial district working as a compliance associate, but it didn't feel right. It was a great opportunity to start out in the business world and acquire some experience until I could find another direction to follow. In my search for something more exciting, I found my way into the sales world of the fashion industry. I sold children's clothes made by iconic brands such as Nike and Levi's before eventually selling clothing and accessories for Liz Claiborne, Juicy Couture and Lucky Brand. Some of it was fun but most of it was still an office job with many hours behind a computer screen and with limited person-to-person contact. Deep down I knew this wasn't for me either.

In 2010, I was forced to take a hard look at what I wanted to do with my life. I realized that the feeling of wanting to be my own boss, that had begun back in Manhattan College, had never left me. I thought of perhaps teaching languages, of becoming a lawyer or of opening my own fashion boutique. My ideas seemed all over the place but I realized that I loved being in touch with emotions and helping people express them. I wanted to work with a variety of people face-to-face, travel, be artistic, creative and allow my analytical side to take care of the business part of it all. As destiny would have it, a photographer friend recommended taking up wedding photography. Bingo. That was it! Pieces of the puzzle seemed to fit. I loved the idea of being trusted to document a couple's most important day, recording their emotions and providing for my own family all at the same time.

I looked back to where I came from and realized that Ecuador is full of entrepreneurs and hard-working people who just do not have the same opportunities that we have here in the United States. Despite the difficulties in Ecuador, I grew up watching people fearlessly follow their dreams and work hard to provide for their families. My grandparents worked night and day to pull their families out of poverty in Ecuador and that work ethic taught my father to also push forward, always in search of a better future. Now it was my turn to provide for my own beautiful little girls and I had the chance to do so by doing something fun and exciting.

I began my research by reading books on wedding photography. Before long I fell in love with it even more. In May of 2010, I bought a semi-pro SLR Nikon D90 camera and continued learning from every resource at my fingertips. I did online research, took online classes, took live classes and even took mentoring sessions with local photographers. I photographed anything and everything I could. In a year, I had outgrown my semi-pro camera and upgraded to my professional Nikon D700 camera with the best quality lenses out there. That year, I continued networking, shooting subjects using two photographers, taking advanced workshops, building my portfolio, and meeting amazing award-winning photographers. I found that, just as when I had gone back to Manhattan College to obtain my degree, I now had a purpose and a goal that made me more determined than ever. With each photography technique I learned and acquired, I made sure to know it so well as to make it my own, so that when I was photographing my clients, I wouldn't even think about the execution of the technique. I simply let my heart take over and I was free to connect with my clients on a personal level. By March of 2012, I was ready to make it official and launch my own business as Jessica Crespo Photography.

For me, life became so much better once I stopped trying to fit in and be someone I wasn't. Today, I live my life the way I want to live it. I love meeting new people and I continue to network, not only with other photographers but with business people in other industries, thanks to Business Guild 2. I also continue training and developing my craft by studying from international award-winning photographers and

Jessica Crespo, who is fluent in three languages, grew up traveling back and forth between the United States and South America. She is adventurous, fun loving and easy going, and she enjoys learning about different cultures. Jessica loves the art of storytelling through images and continuously studies with international photography masters. contact@jessicacrespo.com attending photography conventions. I know I am still at the beginning of my career, but I feel quite accomplished just to be where I am today and to know the direction in which I am going.

From the outside, it may seem like I went around in circles before arriving to where I am now, but that's life. Facing and overcoming obstacles are what have made me more resilient and stronger. Like my parents, I believe in hard work, seeing the good in people and being kind to others. My experiences taught me the importance of having a purpose and of setting goals. Through it all, I learned that I don't need to fit in or settle. Instead, I'm true to who I am by keeping my mind and heart open to new possibilities and positive experiences.

Being a photographer and an entrepreneur allows me the freedom to be creative and to decide how I want to earn my living. I am happy to be a busy working mom with the flexibility to set my own hours. I know I have much more to learn, but I think the key is that we always stay in tune with what makes us happy. My path of self-discovery is not over by any means. As I look forward to continuing to work and grow as an artist and as a professional, I also look forward to passing on the lessons I learned to my own children so they can stay in tune with what makes them happy. Hopefully they, too, will have success of making a career out of their passion.

Thomas King
Advance Lock & Key

Good People Believe

I'll bet it's not every 16-year-old's dream job, but when Jim Devaney offered to let me sweep the floors of his locksmith shop after school, I was unreasonably excited. He lived upstairs in the same apartment building in which I lived with my parents, two brothers and sister. My parents had emigrated from Ireland, with dreams of a better life for their children here in New York.

Mr. Devaney owned J. Devaney Lock & Radio Shop, a small store at Sterling Place and Nostrand Avenue in Brooklyn. I was a student at John Jay High School. I showed up to the lock shop every day after school and swept. I had to take three buses each way to get from school to his shop. But I went each day and swept because it was an opportunity for me. One day, Mr. Devaney let me fix things around the shop. Before long, he taught me how to cut keys. His lessons turned into a full, unpaid apprenticeship for two years. I was eager to learn everything he could possibly teach me about locksmithing. I considered myself lucky that he decided to bring me into his business. At that time, you could only get a good job if your father was in the business or if you knew someone. Neither applied to me. I knew I was given an opportunity that required genuine hard work. With two years of apprenticeship behind me, the next step was to apply for my locksmith license. The committee that oversaw the licensure insisted that I appear before them, unconvinced that at the age of 18 I was mature enough to hold the license. Mr. Devaney vouched for me, and that voucher was all the confidence that I needed. I got the license.

So, with license in hand, I headed into Manhattan and I eventually found a job working for a busy locksmith who had a good reputation. What I did every day was now considered a specialty in Manhattan. I knew I had the best education in the industry. I gained a lot of experience in Manhattan, opening everything from handcuffs to airplanes. For the next eight years I honed my craft and I excelled, but eventually I knew it was time to start out on my own.

I chose the South Shore of Staten Island in which to open my own shop. I gave careful attention to the name I would use and how I would advertise. I knew I wanted to be a permanent staple on the Island. There was no other locksmith on Hylan Boulevard in 1969 and I realized the growth potential at that location. My plan was to put a small shop on the corner of Hylan Boulevard and New Dorp Lane. Only problem was a Bohack supermarket and a skating rink stood in my way on that very same corner. It took quite a bit of convincing before I made the landlord finally understand my vision. He partitioned off 130 square feet that was the entrance to the old skating rink. Business was good. Every person who walked through the doors helped me grow. That was where Advance Lock & Key and my 24-hour service were born. I worked in my small shop during the day and went out on calls in the evening. It was exciting, and my great love of the work never faded.

As my business and inventory grew, I moved the safes outside to the sidewalk during shop hours so that I'd have enough room to get into the store to work. Before long, I outgrew the tiny shop. I moved to a bigger store around the corner—in a shopping center next to the Hylan Cinema. I thrived there for about 10 years, but when my rent went up, I decided it was time to buy my own property. Once again, I did my research, but I knew I wanted to stay in the neighborhood. The corner of Hylan Boulevard and Adams Avenue, in neighboring Grant City, would soon become the permanent home of Advance Lock & Key. That's still where I am today.

Since 1983, Advance Lock & Key at 2050 Hylan Boulevard evolved with every change in the market, technology, new developments in the trade and advancements in the industry. As my business continues to evolve, I aim to stay grounded on the old school, small business principles that have kept me alive for four decades.

Every time I think I've seen it all, something else surprises me. In a mere 24 hours, Superstorm Sandy all but destroyed a thriving business that took me 43 years to build. The shop was destroyed—but my business wasn't. I learned something very humbling after the storm: that the good people of Staten Island believed in my *business*, not in my *shop*. And that

Tom King knows safes and locks inside out. For a break from his emergency service, he and his wife traveled to Maine a few summers ago. thmking5@yahoo.com

was all I needed to know to get back up from that almost-fatal blow.

Advance Lock & Key is part of Staten Island. It always was and always will be. It stays open because of the good people who walk into my shop every day. They need something I can help them with. I'm grateful for the business, the challenge and the ability to get up each day and work hard. I can honestly say I like going into work every day, heading to some sort of new challenge each morning. If I didn't enjoy what I chose to do with my life, I wouldn't have lasted this long. The most fulfillment I get is helping people and being able to give them a good, fair and honest job.

One of the most crucial pieces of advice I learned over the years is that the faith you have in yourself and your business is most important. The faith I've had in my own success has been vital to my business thriving. There were always moments when it didn't feel like the right time to make the big decisions for my business. But I believed in what I was doing and I worked hard to make it succeed—and that's made all the difference.

Relationships
Are
Associations

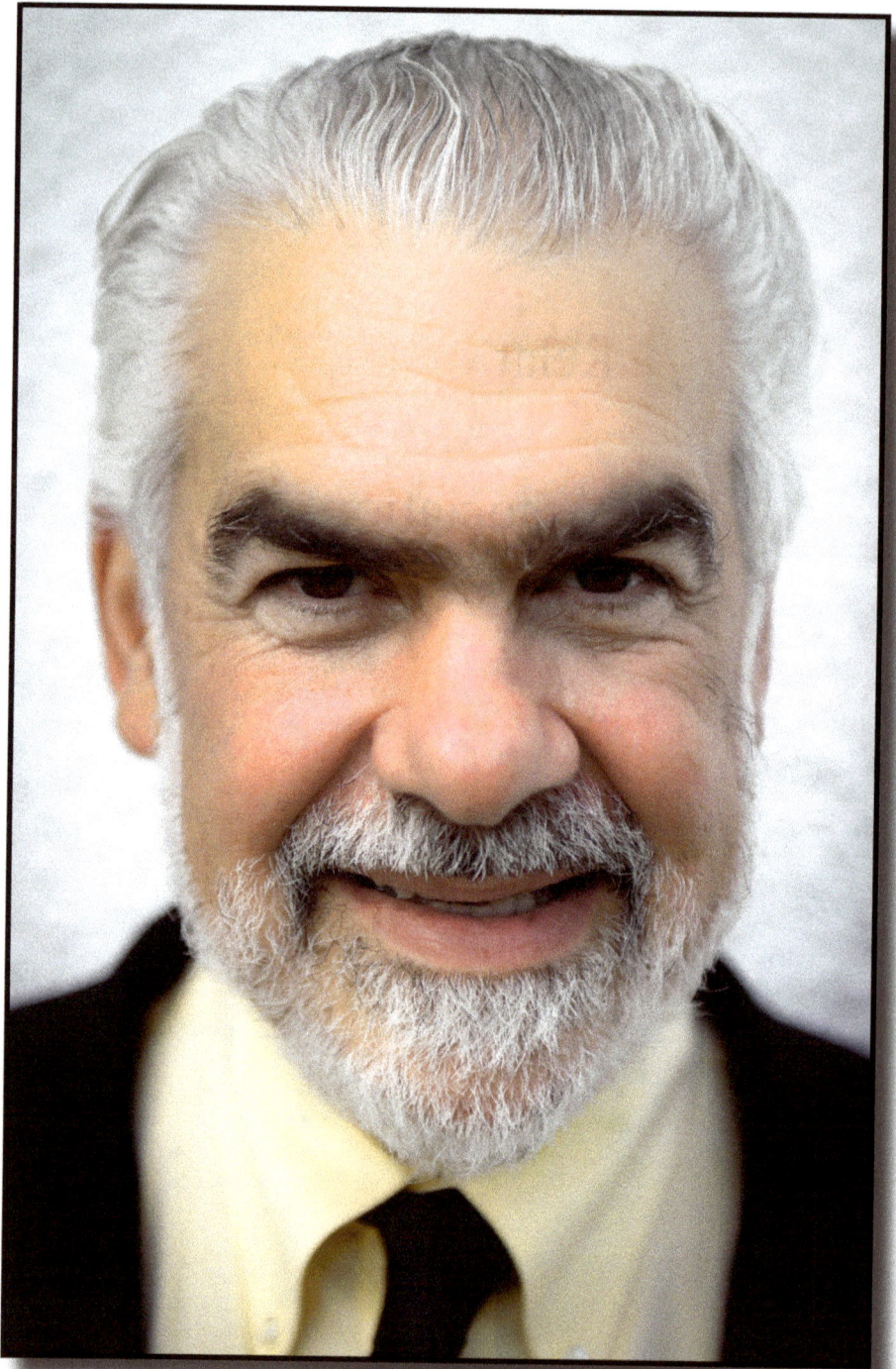

Lou Rizzo
Master Realtors

Interacting with People

I held several jobs in my life. But my goal was to settle comfortably into a long term profession. It was a winding road, but every step of the journey has included a learning opportunity which has enhanced my goal. The most beneficial lesson I have learned, however, is that a career should be fulfilling.

My diverse experience includes adventures as a college student; military tours in the United States, Germany and South Vietnam; work in a psychiatric center; student teaching; operating an ice cream truck; and owning a nightclub. I also tended bar at several Staten Island and New York City establishments. To this day, I still tend bar two nights a week. This side job gives me the opportunity to meet people and to network.

Most of my life's work has been interacting with people. I consider myself a people person, and I truly enjoy socializing and conversing. So when the opportunity to pursue a career in real estate materialized a number of years ago, I took it. I soon realized that in order to be successful at my new real estate career, I needed to put my heart and soul into it. And I would need to build my business in an efficient manner, since I wanted potential clients to look at my new company as one that would be beneficial to work with.

As a licensed associate real estate broker, I am considered an independent contractor. That means I am not paid a salary; instead, I am paid by commission. I have been doing this for more than 20 years. My business involves prospecting for new clients, as well as networking. Getting inventory became a little easier once I became established. However, it was a struggle in the beginning. So, one of the first lessons I learned during my formative years was the art of self-promotion. I also learned computer skills.

The next step, which I considered the most important, was networking. — and establishing *relationships*. I had to make myself known to my family, friends and former customers and clients. I also had to network with other businesses. So one of the first networking opportunities that came my way was to join Business Guild 2 of the Staten Island Chamber of Commerce. I joined the guild about 15 years ago, and I am still a member. About 25 of us meet every Thursday morning to exchange business tips and to share business referrals. I served as guild president and vice president. My association with Business Guild 2 afforded me the opportunity to give and receive business contacts. In fact, there were years when my real estate business was slow, yet referrals to me from other guild members accounted for at least half my business.

Through the guild, I learned many important skills. For example, I learned to turn social situations into networking opportunities. Sometimes we meet with other business groups. When that occurs, I take the time to introduce myself to someone I have not met previously. I engage the person in a conversation, and we exchange business cards. Then, I move on to someone else to do the same thing. I made many business connections this way.

I also learned to explain my profession without overselling myself, but by creating a situation where people want to know more about me. This is achieved by my serving as a source of information about everything that relates to my profession — real estate. When I help someone to buy or sell a house, I want to be their Realtor for life. I want them to call me anytime they have questions about anything relating to real estate. When questions or challenges outside of my area of expertise arise, my solution is to recommend other professionals within my business circle who are experts in the area of concern. I do so with full confidence because I trust those in my professional circle.

I learned, too, to treat business referrals with the respect. If I am being referred by a colleague, I am a reflection of that person. As a result, I always give referrals priority. I also send the person who gave me the referral a thank you card, or I give him or her an appreciative phone call. You see, I believe getting new customers is a full time job. Referrals, therefore, are a great and easier way to accomplish this.

I still tend bar and I am a Staten Island Ski Club member. Both offer me opportunities to meet and talk to people. So between bartending, guild membership and ski club membership, I meet and talk to a lot of people!

Here's an interesting story that illustrates what I mean. One day as I was bartending, I couldn't help but overhearing a couple discussing their upcoming marriage. My ears perked up! The guy suggested that if they get married, his future wife would have to sell her house, and he would have to sell his house. They would then pool their money and buy a larger house. Bingo! Or so I thought. Then I hear him say he would never hire a real estate agent because they were all crooked. I was still listening. Then he ordered a drink. Instead of placing his drink in front of him, I placed my business card there. Well, he knew I had heard the whole conversation. I served him his cocktail and engaged him in conversation. And it was a pleasant conversation at that. The end result: I helped him sell his house — and his future wife's house as well! I was also able to help them buy a $750,000 house — one of my listings. That was a total of four transactions and a lasting friendship.

Now, my ski club relationships. Over the years I have gone on many ski trips. I go at least twice a year. I wind up spending a whole week with other members. While we ski and enjoy each other's company, we also wind up discussing our professions. Many of these ski trip relationships led to lucrative business opportunities. I represented dozens of my friends and ski buddies when the time came for them to sell or buy their homes. And, believe me, my initial intention on a ski trip is to relax and enjoy. But business always seems to come up casually, and I follow up.

So, no matter the profession you are in, I recommend networking. This advice is particularly sage for those who provide a service or are sales focused. There are many ways to do so; joining a networking group is an excellent way.

Others that I try to assist through networking are veterans groups. As a returning Vietnam veteran, I am sympathetic to soldiers' needs when they return to civilian life.

I realize times were different when I served in the military, and thankfully the public is much more accepting of veterans now than during the Vietnam War years. But, the situation is similar as far as finances go. I promised myself that when veterans return home these days, they should never be treated like they were treated after the unpopular Vietnam War. A returning veteran usually needs as much help as possible to settle into a normal civilian life. Many programs exist to help them when they decide to start a family and buy their first house. Today I work closely with a mortgage professional in my networking group to learn more about veteran loans, and I have become proficient at helping returning veterans.

In closing, I suggest choosing a job you will enjoy. If you are in business for yourself, it should be part of your lifestyle. Going to work should be exciting. But remember, no matter what you do, give it your all. Just because you enjoy it today, does not mean it will be easy all the time. There will undoubtedly be difficult times. While going to work should be easy, there will be difficult times. And whether it is an easy day or a difficult one, remember to take care of your present and former clients while prospecting and networking for new ones. And when you receive a referral through networking, always remember to thank the person who gave you the referral.

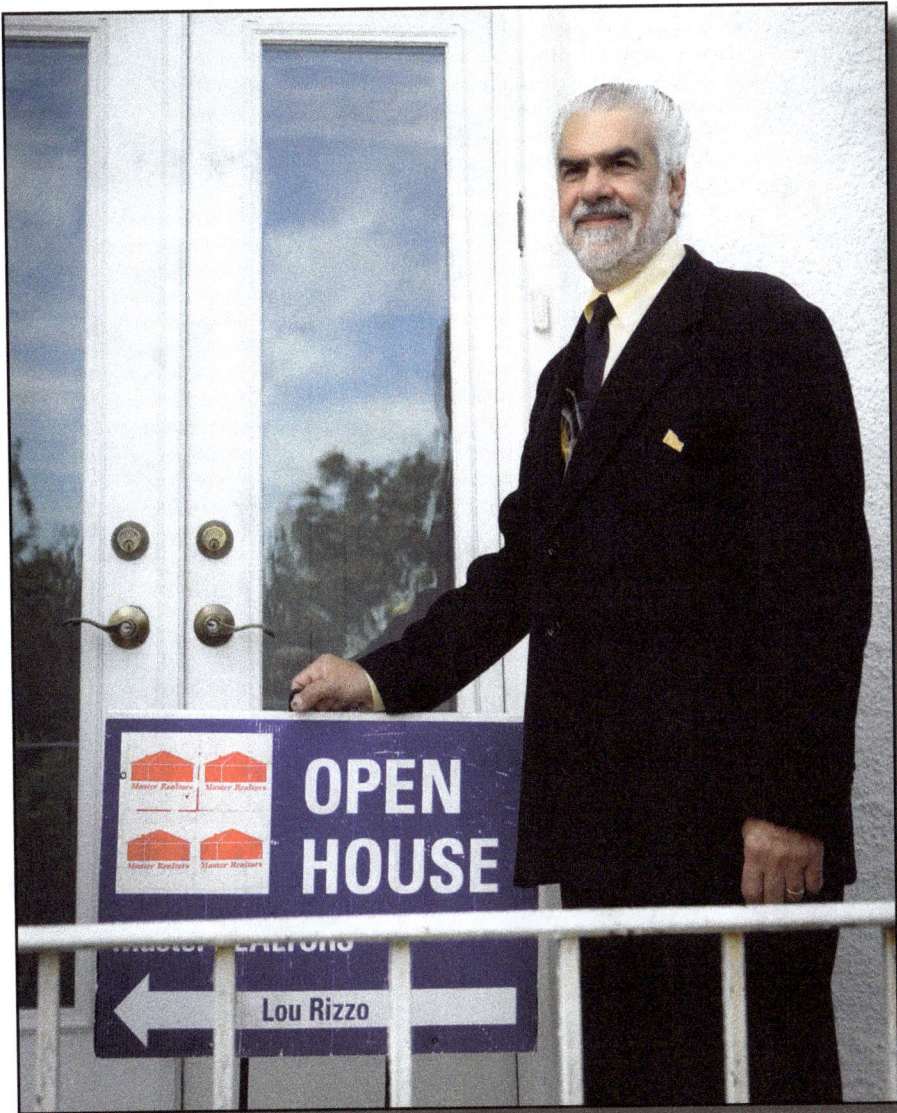

Lou Rizzo has assisted buyers and sellers in real estate for the past 15 years. Lou is an avid skier and Staten Island Ski Club member, and has a passion to follow the New York Yankees when they're on the road. lou@lrizzo.com

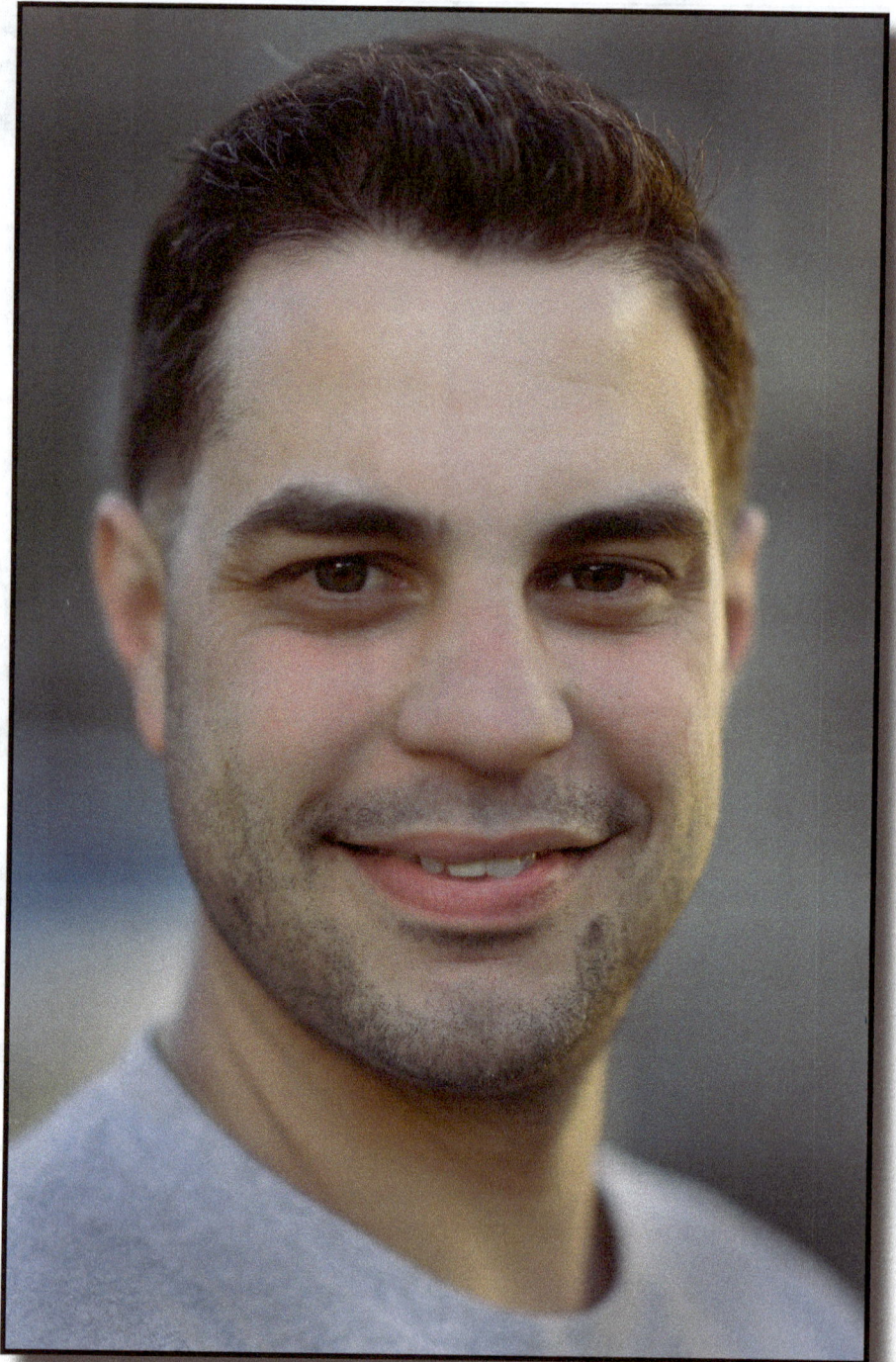

Stephen Molloy
Molloy Electric

Benefits of Networking

It's not easy being green, Kermit the Frog likes to say. Nor is it easy launching a new business. I can tell you first hand that a business owner is apt to encounter a wide variety of problems. But in trying to solve these many problems I must tell you I have found that networking and establishing *relationships* is a positive way to increase clientele, add new vendors and meet other successful business owners.

Before I went into business for myself, I was a member of Local 3 of the International Brotherhood of Electrical Workers. As a union member, I worked for a firm that performed most of the electrical maintenance at the South Street Seaport in Lower Manhattan. It was there that I met a group of great people. I began to grow. Unbeknownst to me, I was actually networking and developing relationships. My first client, Tom, owned Clipper City, a beautiful-looking schooner built in 1854 that today cruises New York harbor. Clipper City is docked at South Street Seaport so I performed the off shore power, and all electrical work on the boat. As our relationship grew Tom introduced me to Dan, from the company Rapid Park. Before long Rapid Park became one of my best accounts.

My first meeting with Dan was more like a couple of old friends shooting the breeze, rather than like an introduction meeting. Dan was an eager businessman who was willing to give me names and contacts of potential clients. One potential client in particular was Peter, who works with energy efficiency in New York City. Peter is a happy full-of-life type guy who wants to see everyone around him succeed. I was lucky to have met Peter. He shared his knowledge of conserving energy for businesses on a corporate level. It was then I knew I would be able to branch out on my own with the help of my small network of driven individuals who inspired me to become a successful business owner, as I had always dreamed.

After a year on my own I realized just how hard it was to own and operate a business. My only background was that of an electrician. I had no business background. Consequently, the business part did not come easy. But that's where my most important relationship came into play. A year earlier I passed my business card to Henry at a meeting. Now, Henry proposed a project with which he needed help. We met — and a relationship mushroomed. Henry was willing to share with me the experiences and secrets of how he ran his electrical contracting company successfully for more than 35 years. He was like a breath of fresh air. He was the mentor I needed. For two straight years I worked side by side with Henry, and I absorbed as much as I could. Then it was my time to go out on my own, using everything I learned. Henry and I are lifelong friends who continue to work together to this day!

Now it was time to hit the pavement and get the word out about my firm, Molloy Electric. Luckily I know some people who introduced me to the technique of networking and to networking groups. One day a friend invited me to my first local networking event. It seemed easy! Apparently all I had to do was mingle with other business owners and talk about my work. I figured I could easily do that. And so I did. Before long I realized this would be a good way to meet small business owners like myself. One group I was impressed with was the Greenbelt Conservancy, a non-for-profit organization that worked to care for the Staten Island community and the borough's hundreds of acres of parks, trails and open spaces. My dream for Molloy Electric is to eventually give back to my community by helping others. I would like to help as many people as I can — just as these past relationships helped me.

Another constant struggle I had day in and day out was finding good workers. I placed advertisements on websites for experienced men and women. But the ads only brought me people who were not willing to devote the necessary time to the job. Or they brought me workers who would show up one day and not show up the next day. At this point I needed a new route, so I turned to my small business network to help get the word out. I was looking for an eager learner or learners willing to learn the electrical business my way — which I know is the correct way. I sought someone I could teach the secrets and skills that I was taught. After being in contact with many people, fellow business owners, friends and family, I received a call one day from an experienced electrician

Stephen Molloy is so consumed with his electrical contracting business that he has hardly any time for anything else. stephen@molloyelectric.com.

who said he needed work. Funny how he got my information. My uncle who rode the Staten Island Ferry every day for work was talking to a fellow passenger about how hard it was to find employment. One story led to another and it turned out this man's son was an experienced electrician who was having a hard time finding work. I hired him. After his first day on the job I knew he would be a good fit. Before attending the small business events I never thought of using networking as a way to find employees but, as I learned, networking has many benefits.

My electrical business has thrived on networking and relationships. I am certainly appreciative to the various small business groups that make it possible for me to meet people who impact my thinking as a small business owner.

Dovid Winiarz
Fidelity Payment Services

Four Secrets to Success

I am sitting down at a clean desk.

I am sitting down to put into writing my secrets to success in the workforce. Why, you ask, am I willing to share my secrets? I am willing to share my secrets because I do not believe anything can ever be taken from me unless I deserve for it to be taken from me. It is my hope that my sharing with you will merit my being deserving of you wanting to give back.

That may sound selfish but it's simply good business practice. As a Torah observant Jew who interacts with the world at large, I am always careful to give, as appropriate, without hope for recompense until after I die, because heavenly reward is always better for an eternity. That being said, I am hopeful for a long and productive life, and that requires executing sound business practices.

As I said, I am sitting down at a clean desk.

I took the time to stack my piles of chaos into neat stacks and organize them according to importance because that is Secret Number One of how to be successful.

What is the lesson, you ask? Don't be afraid to make the mess because cleaning up may interrupt your creative flow. But, remember, you must clean up after yourself. Better yet, hire someone to do it for you. I have found that if you don't have a good assistant, you will wind up being that assistant yourself. What is the dollar value you put on yourself and on your time? Are you worth $300,000 a year? $500,000? What is that magic number that would make you feel as if you are a financial success?

Be real, but think highly of yourself. When you look in the mirror and remember that you were created in G-d's[1] image, your estimation of

---

1 You may be wondering why I refer to Him as G-d—with a dash. Here's the reason. In Jewish literature His name completely elevates the paper on which it is printed to the point where that paper could not be disposed of in the traditional way, such as throwing it out in the garbage. It would have to be disposed of differently. Writing with the dash eliminates that problem. The rest of this book may not need this

your value should skyrocket. Let us assume you want to earn $365,000 a year. How many hours a week and how many weeks out of the year do you want to work? Again, be real, but make sure to leave time for G-d and family. Let us say you want to work 49 weeks a year and not more than 45 hours a week. $350,000 divided by 49 weeks puts your financial worth at $7,142.86 a week. Divide that by 45 hours and you are worth (in the financial arena) $158.73 an hour.

So, if you become your own assistant, you are losing $158.73 every hour you spend doing tasks you could delegate. So make the mess if you must but don't be afraid to pay someone $10 or $15 an hour to clean it up.

That is Secret Number One.

Secret Number Two came about when I worked for Leona Helmsley more than 25 years ago. I am scratching my head trying to figure out how it is possible that I was in the work force 25 years ago, but I guess staying alive will do that to you. Leona Helmsley, you may recall, was married to real estate magnate Harry Helmsley, and was a shrewd businesswoman in her own right.

She taught me something that is commonplace in the business world today, but only because people like her drilled it into us back then. "Always offer it to the guy next door first," she told us. Whatever product you are promoting, chances are the guy next door has the most vested interest in acquiring it.

I actually put this creed into practice one day when I walked into a warehouse in Edison, N.J., and walked out an hour later with an exclusive right to represent the occupant in subleasing his 50,000 sq. ft. warehouse. Remembering what I had been taught, I crossed the parking lot before getting in my car and walked into the building next door instead. When I succeeded in connecting with the tenant there, he informed me that he desperately needed to expand but his landlord refused to let him out of his lease to rent the additional square footage he needed. At this point I am sure I could have signed him up on the spot for the privilege of sub-leasing his space as well. Instead, I asked him how much space he needed to grow his company. As you can imagine I was delighted to hear that he needed between 50,000 and 55,000 square feet. When I asked him if he would consider the building on the other side of the parking lot, he responded, "Larry's space? He doesn't have anything available."

treatment because it is not a Jewish Book. In my story, however, I write it this way because I subscribe to this value system. Finally, I'm happy to use this opportunity as a delightful teaching moment because you may have just learned something new.

I asked him why he thought that and he quickly retorted, "Are you kidding? We play golf every Wednesday. He would've said something to me."

Suffice it to say, Larry was not too pleased about paying me the $25,000 commission for the five-year lease his golf buddy signed. But Leona Helmsley and I were pleased as punch. Always offer it to the guy next door first.

As I mentioned earlier, I am a Torah observant Jew and I always appreciate the opportunity to highlight how good business practice, as well as anything else good in life, has discussion value from the Torah. There is a story about a Rabbi who saw a congregant running. He asked him where he was going. The congregant replied, "I'm running to earn a living." With a warm smile, the Rabbi took his hand and asked: "So tell me, how do you know you are not running in the wrong direction?"

A famous person once said that the harder you work the luckier you become. While this is certainly true to an extent, the Torah teaches that we are "given permission" to put our faith in whatever we want. If we put our faith in our own capabilities, sadly, eventually they will fail us, if only because of our advanced age. If we put our faith in politicians, we will need to rely on them. The successful businessperson puts his faith in G-d, that He will provide the right opportunities for us to earn a living. Since G-d is everywhere, why run all over?

Always offer it to the guy next door first. If you deserve the reward, the guy next door will want it and you can go home early.

Working with Mrs. Helmsley always provided me with nuggets of wisdom that I apply to my business practice to this day.

Secret Number Three follows: I remember her teaching us to always tell people what you do. Sounds pretty straightforward but you would be amazed how many people I meet at networking events who fail to tell me what they do for a living or how I could help them. They do not even bring a business card to hand out. "Oh, I'm sorry, I forgot to bring cards..." is a refrain I hear at least twice at every single event I have ever attended in more than 26 years.

"Always tell people what you do" is what allowed me to do business with a toll collector at the Verrazano-Narrows Bridge.

"Always tell people what you do" is what allowed me to help a 17-year-old kid to get the house he had inherited taken care of by an estate attorney with whom I worked.

"Always tell people what you do" is what allowed me to sign up a client from a Facebook posting—which led to three more referrals!

"Always tell people what you do" is what allowed me to do business with the mailman who handled my mail at the local post office. I never met him until he called me one day because of a sticker I put on the outside of a bill I was mailing. The sticker explained what I did!

Secret Number Four, and with this I will close, is the secret I taught Leona. My name is Dovid. My email is Dovid@Dovid.com. As you can imagine, I am proud of my name. I am so proud of my name that when my boss, Mrs. Helmsley, told me that I would "lose business" if I did not use a more generic name like David on my business cards, I refused.

Several months later, I landed an account from a Mr. Kaufman. Mrs. Helmsley wanted to know how I landed the account that the office had been pursuing for months before I came on board. Here's how: Mr. Kaufman had explained that his name was Harold. But his given name was Chaim. He went by Harold because his mother always told him that he would "lose business" if he used his real, "more exotic" name. When Chaim finally met someone—me—who was not ashamed to be himself, and who even used his real name on his business card, that was the person to whom he would give his business!

Secret Number Four, that Leona Rosenberg Helmsley learned from a 22-year-old proud and Jewish-American businessman, was that in order to succeed, you always have to be proud of who you are and Whom you represent.

Success, in the final analysis, is not how much you put in the bank or how many toys you have, but who you are when you look in the mirror. You were created in G-d's image; if you see that image looking back at you … you are a success!

Dovid Winiarz contributed this story to the book
"From Humble Beginnings ... Success"
published in 2013. It is being reprinted here
because it is relevant to business relationships.

Dovid Winiarz died in an automobile collision
shortly after the publication of "Success."

Dovid Winiarz is a businessman and rabbi who likes to help people. He wears many different hats or, if you prefer, yarmulkes. To find out what Dovid is up to now, shoot him an email at dovid@dovid.com, call him at 718-983-9272 or locate him on Linked In at www.linkedin.com/in/dovidwiniarz. Friend him there. But reach out to him as well to really get to know him. He says he'd love to know you.

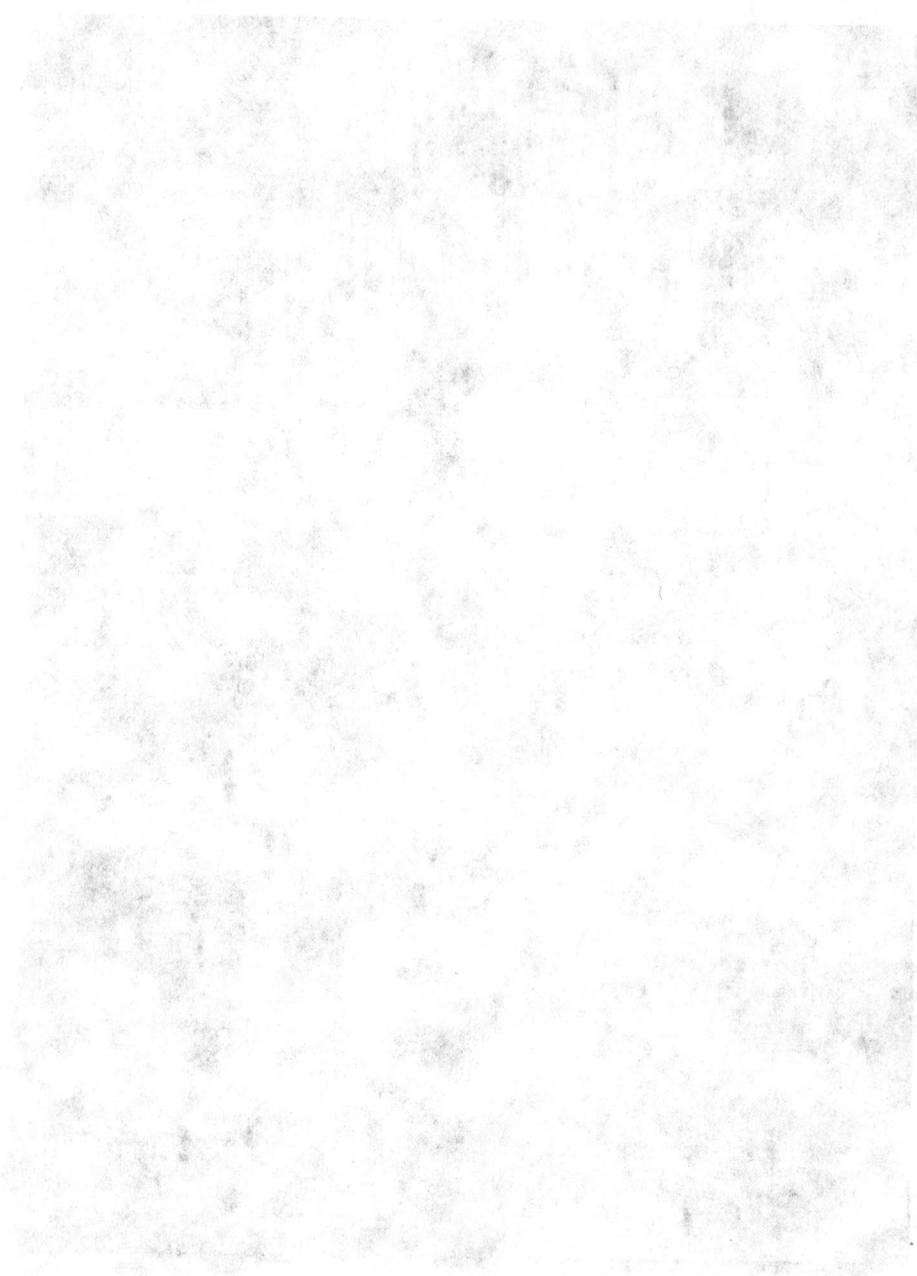

www.ingramcontent.com/pod-product-compliance
Lightning Source LLC
Chambersburg PA
CBHW052016230326
41598CB00078B/3522